VAJRAYANA

An Essential Guide to Practice

Books by Traleg Kyabgon

Actuality of Being: Dzogchen and Tantric Perspectives, Shogam Publications, 2020

Desire: Why It Matters, Shogam Publications, 2019

Integral Buddhism: Developing All Aspects of One's Personhood, Shogam Publications, 2018

King Doha: Saraha's Advice to a King, Shogam Publications, 2018

Letter to a Friend: Nagarjuna's Classic Text, Shogam Publications, 2018

Song of Karmapa: The Aspiration of the Mahamudra of True Meaning by Lord Rangjung Dorje, Shogam Publications, 2018

Moonbeams of Mahamudra: The Classic Meditation Manual, Shogam Publications, 2015

Karma: What it is, What it isn't, and Why it matters, Shambhala Publications, 2015

Four Dharmas of Gampopa, KTD Publications, 2013

Asanga's Abhidharmasamuccaya, KTD Publications, 2013

Ninth Karmapa Wangchuk Dorje's Ocean Of Certainty, KTD Publications, 2011

Influence of Yogacara on Mahamudra, KTD Publications, 2010

The Practice of Lojong: Cultivating Compassion through Training the Mind, Shambhala Publications, 2007

Mind at Ease: Self-Liberation through Mahamudra Meditation, Shambhala Publications, 2004

Benevolent Mind: A Manual in Mind Training, Zhyisil Chokyi Ghatsal Publications, 2003

Photo facing page: Traleg Kyabgon Rinpoche the Ninth

VAJRAYANA
An Essential Guide to Practice

Traleg Kyabgon

Foreword by Dzigar Kongtrül Rinpoche

SHOGAM
PUBLICATIONS
2020

Shogam Publications Pty Ltd
PO Box 239 Ballarat Central
Victoria, Australia, 3353
www.shogam.org
info@shogam.com

Printed in Australia and the United States of America

Edited by Salvatore Celiento

Designed by David Bennett

Library Reference
Kyabgon, Traleg, 1955
Desire: Why It Matters

Printed book ISBN: 978-0-6483321-52 (Paperback)
E-book ISBN: 978-0-6483321-69

DEDICATION

Dedicated to all mother sentient beings

Contents

Foreword

Through the ages masters of the Vajrayana lineage have secretly and profoundly kept the teachings alive and vibrant for those in future generations. This has allowed them to bestow empowerments, teachings, and pith instructions with the same vitality that they themselves received from their own masters. Now, even in the 21st century after many centuries and stretching over a millennia, we still have the profound opportunity to receive the blessings of and be greatly benefited by the initial teachings of Buddha Vajradhara.

Traleg Kyabgon Rinpoche is one of these masters who kept the Vajrayana teachings vibrant and alive. With his immense wisdom and deep compassion for all living beings, his whole life's legacy has been to transmit and transplant the dharma, particularly the Vajrayana lineage, into the new frontier of the western world. He has kindly given many teachings on the various Vajrayana subjects contained in this book in order to support and enhance our practice. These teachings illuminate the tantra and open up the meaning so we may access and fully appreciate what would otherwise remain hidden.

Felicity, Traleg Kyabgon Rinpoche's Khandro, and all his students, have done an amazing job to keep Rinpoche's teachings in the world by transcribing, editing, and publishing books like this. Their work is invaluable to all who have a connection to the Vajrayana dharma and especially to those connected to the Nyingma and Kagyu lineages. I therefore thank them and am immensely grateful for their dedication and devotion.

Dzigar Kongtrül Rinpoche

Biography of Author
TRALEG KYABGON RINPOCHE IX

Traleg Kyabgon Rinpoche IX (1955-2012) was born in Nangchen in Kham, eastern Tibet. He was recognized by His Holiness XVI Gyalwang Karmapa as the ninth Traleg tulku and enthroned at the age of two as the supreme abbot of Thrangu Monastery. Rinpoche was taken to Rumtek Monastery in Sikkim at the age of four where he was educated with other young tulkus in exile by His Holiness Karmapa for the next five years.

Rinpoche began his studies under the auspices of His Eminence Kyabje Thuksey Rinpoche at Sangngak Choling in Darjeeling. He also studied with a number of other eminent Tibetan teachers during that time and mastered the many Tibetan teachings with the Kagyu and Nyingma traditions in particular, including the *Havajra Tantra*, *Guhyasamaja Tantra*, and the third Karmapa's *Zabmo Nangdon* (*The Profound Inner Meaning*) under Khenpo Noryang (abbot of Sangngak Choling). Rinpoche studied the *Abhidharmakosha*, *Pramanavarttika*, *Bodhisattvacharyavatara*, *Abhidharmasamuccaya*, *Six Treaties of Nagarjuna*, the *Madhyanta-vibhaga*, and the *Mahayanuttaratantra* with Khenpo Sogyal. He also studied with Khenpo Sodar and was trained in tantric ritual practices by Lama Ganga, who had been specifically sent by His Holiness Karmapa for that purpose.

In 1967 Rinpoche moved to the Institute of Higher Tibetan Studies in Sarnath, and studied extensively for the next five years. He studied Buddhist history, Sanskrit, and Hindi, as well as Longchenpa's *Finding Comfort and Ease* (*Ngalso Korsum*), *Seven Treasuries* (*Longchen Dzod Dun*), *Three Cycles of Liberation* (*Rangdrol Korsum*), and *Longchen Nyingthig* with Khenchen Palden Sherab Rinpoche and Khenpo Tsondru.

When Rinpoche had completed these studies at the age of

sixteen, he was sent by His Holiness Karmapa to study under the auspices of the Venerable Khenpo Yesha Chodar at Sanskrit University in Varanasi for three years. Rinpoche was also tutored by khenpos and geshes from all four traditions of Tibetan Buddhism during this time.

Rinpoche was subsequently put in charge of Zangdog Palri Monastery (the glorious copper colored mountain) in Eastern Bhutan and placed under the private tutelage of Dregung Khenpo Ngedon by His Holiness Karmapa to continue his studies of Sutra and Tantra. He ran this monastery for the next three years and began learning English during this time.

From 1977 to 1980, Rinpoche returned to Rumtek in Sikkim to fill the honored position of His Holiness' translator, where he dealt with many English-speaking Western visitors.

Rinpoche moved to Melbourne, Australia in 1980 and commenced studies in comparative religion and philosophy at LaTrobe University. Rinpoche established E-Vam Institute in Melbourne in 1982 and went on to establish further Centers in Australia, America, and New Zealand. For the next 25 years Rinpoche gave weekly teachings, intensive weekend courses, and retreats on classic Kagyu and Nyingma texts. During this time Rinpoche also taught internationally travelling extensively through America, Europe, and South East Asia and was appointed the Spiritual Director of Kamalashila Institute in Germany for five years in the 1980's.

Rinpoche established a retreat center, Maitripa Centre in Healesville, Australia in 1997 where he conducted two public retreats a year. Rinpoche founded E-Vam Buddhist Institute in the U.S in 2000, and Nyima Tashi Buddhist Centre in New Zealand in 2004. In 2010 Rinpoche established a Buddhist college called Shogam Vidhalaya at E-Vam Institute in Australia and instructed students on a weekly basis.

Throughout his life Rinpoche gave extensive teachings on many aspects of Buddhist psychology and philosophy, as well as comparative religion, and Buddhist and Western thought. He was an active writer and has many titles to his name. Titles include: the best selling *Essence of Buddhism*; *Karma, What It Is, What It Isn't, and Why It Matters*; *The Practice of Lojong*; *Moonbeams of Mahamudra*; and many more. Many of Rinpoche's books are translated into a number of different languages including Chinese, French, German, Korean, and Spanish. Rinpoche's writings are thought provoking, challenging, profound, and highly relevant to today's world and its many challenges.

Rinpoche was active in publishing during the last two decades of his life, beginning with his quarterly magazine *Ordinary Mind*, which ran from 1997 to 2003. Further, Rinpoche founded his own publishing arm Shogam Publications in 2008 and released a number of books on Buddhist history, philosophy, and psychology and left instructions for the continuation of this vision. His vision for Shogam and list of titles can be found at www.shogam.com.

Rinpoche's ecumenical approach can be seen in his other activities aimed at bringing buddhadharma to the West. He established the biannual Buddhism and Psychotherapy Conference (1994 - 2003), and Tibet Here and Now Conference (2005), and the annual Buddhist Summer School (1984 to the present).

Traleg Kyabgon Rinpoche IX passed into parinirvana on 24 July 2012, on Chokhor Duchen, the auspicious day of the Buddha's first teaching. Rinpoche stayed in meditation (*thugdam*) for weeks after his passing. A traditional cremation ceremony was conducted at Maitripa Centre and a stupa was erected on the center's grounds in Rinpoche's honor.

It is a privilege to continue Rinpoche's vision and initiatives, and to continue to make the profound teachings of Traleg Kyabgon Rinpoche IX given in the West for over 30 years available through his Centers' activities and Shogam Publications. Rinpoche's Sangha hope that many will benefit.

Acknowledgements

First and foremost many thanks must go to Traleg Kyabgon Rinpoche the Ninth for the precious gift of these profound teachings. Thank you to Traleg Khandro for assisting in understanding the meaning of Traleg Rinpoche's precious, vast, and incredible words. Thank you to Jampa Dhadrak La for his expert guidance on the Tibetan and Sanskrit terms used by Traleg Rinpoche. Thanks to David Bennett who designed and formatted the book and also created the beautiful cover.

Salvatore Celiento

Editor's Introduction

As is the case with all of Traleg Kyabgon Rinpoche the Ninth's teachings, this book will very likely change or even radically transform a practitioner's meditation practice and conceptual understanding of Buddhism. The teachings within explain how to practice esoteric Buddhism so that one can internalize them to make use of the transformative qualities of the different tantric practices. I believe it is an extremely important work for anyone interested in such practices.

These teachings given so generously by Traleg Rinpoche are a collection of three courses given at different periods of time. In part one, Rinpoche covers an overview of Tantra while elucidating key tantric concepts. Toward the end of part one, Rinpoche introduces the Six Yogas of Naropa within the context of the overview, and in part two, Rinpoche explores the Six Yogas of Naropa in more depth. Here, Rinpoche gives vital information and explanations regarding how to understand and practice these most esoteric practices. In part three, Rinpoche delves more deeply into the philosophy and practice of dream yoga, one of the Six Yogas. Rinpoche's clear explanations of key points allow for a subtle and nuanced understanding of ordinarily mystifying tantric concepts. Indeed, this text is an extremely sophisticated, subtle, and profound elucidation of ideas that have traditionally been shrouded in obscure and confusing language.

I hope this book will provide immense benefit to experienced and new students of Tibetan Buddhism, practitioners of meditation, philosophers, academics, and those who wish to explore the vast and profound esoteric practices described by one of the foremost masters of Tibetan Buddhism, Traleg Kyabgon Rinpoche the Ninth.

Salvatore Celiento
Shogam Publications

VAJRAYANA

An Essential Guide to Practice

Overview of Buddhist Tantra

Chapter One

Sutra and Tantra: Differences Between Exoteric and Esoteric Buddhism

To understand Tibetan Buddhism, it is best to have some understanding of Buddhist Tantra even if one does not perform tantric practices. It can be easy in the western environment to engage in tantric practices such as deity yoga without sufficient information available on its significance. Commentarial material in the corpus of the Buddhist canon and that authored by native Tibetan masters is not necessarily easily accessible.

In Tibet, Buddhist Tantra is known by many names. The most common term is *gyud*, which means "continuity." This is the Tibetan equivalent for the Sanskrit word "Tantra." In Tibetan, the tantric teachings are also known as *sa ngag* (Skt. *guhya mantra*), which means "secret mantra" or "secret incantation." They are also known as *dorje thegpa* or *vajrayana*, meaning "indestructible vehicle." These types of teachings are referred to as "gyud" or "Tantra" signifying our own Buddha-nature or "the nature of our potential for awakening" is already present in our deluded state, prior to the attainment of enlightenment. There is continuity in the mindstream between the deluded state of being and the state of Buddhahood or awakening. The designation "secret mantra" or "secret incantation" refers to the use of mantras in tantric rituals. These mantras are symbolic representations of deities, which in turn, are manifestations of our true nature. Mantras therefore, are the keys for unlocking the hidden and secret chamber of our true nature. With the use of mantric methods, the secret is revealed.

"Indestructible vehicle" has a similar connotation to the word "Tantra." Our "indestructible" or "vajra" nature refers to our Buddha-nature or true nature. This cannot be destroyed by corruptions, defilements, delusions, or ignorance. All three of these terms refer to our true nature, which has to be seen as the working basis for tantric practices. We need to presuppose belief and conviction in the indestructibility of our own true nature to engage in tantric practice.

In Tantrism, the methods we use and the understandings we must develop are different from those found in the sutric approach. In Tibetan the word for "Sutra" is *mdo*, which has the connotation of "being in a valley," or being more geographically accessible than the crevasses between mountains (Tib. *phu*). The sutric teachings are accessible to all because they are easier to understand, but they are considered more difficult to practice. By contrast, it is said that tantric teachings are hard to understand but easier to practice.

The sutric and tantric teachings are also referred to as "exoteric" and "esoteric" teachings, respectively. Tantra is considered esoteric because it is harder to decode. In fact, tantric language is sometimes referred to as "twilight language" due to the deliberately obscure symbolic nature of its references. Since tantric teachings cannot be taken literally, many different methods are used in Tantra in order to "unpack" the various statements made there to reveal their meaning. The sutric and tantric methods are regarded as complementary in Tibetan Buddhism. There is no contradiction between them. It is not the case that we only do tantric or sutric practices. Sutric practice should be incorporated and integrated into tantric practice.

In both of these traditions, the general understanding is that we, as human beings, have come into this world with great potential. However, in spite of this potential, we are not naturally equipped or endowed to automatically reach it; we have to work at it. According to Buddhist teachings, this is important not only in relation to our present life, but also in relation to our innumerable lives. For since we believe in rebirth, it appears that up to this point, we have never taken the opportunity to reach our true destination, our true calling. We have squandered our lifetimes. If we are not careful and do not become reflective and cultivate ourselves, we are at risk of also squandering the present life. If we simply yield to our whims and impulses and become caught up in our delusory ways of thinking, making no attempt to decrease our level of ignorance and gain knowledge of ourselves, our lives will have been squandered. If we do not want to waste the present life, we can make something of it by utilizing every opportunity to reach our potential. Reaching this potential is not something that we have to achieve by relying on someone else's kindness or good nature. It is something that we can realize by ourselves, for ourselves. To do that, we have to gain self-knowledge. We have to understand ourselves; what our current situation is truly like and what our true potential is.

All Buddhist practices, whether they are sutric and exoteric in nature, or tantric and esoteric in nature, are designed to deal with our present human condition. We do this because according to Buddhism, we are never truly free but always at the mercy of unresolved issues. We are afflicted with anxieties and frustrations, pushed and pulled by varieties of conflicting emotions,[1] and have inculcated all manner of self-destructive habit patterns. We have to learn to deal with these in order to reach our full potential.

According to Buddhism, the goal of our "full potential" consists of total freedom and the endowment of wisdom and insight. As samsaric creatures, we are not considered free; we are considered ignorant. However, we have the potential to become free and enlightened precisely because the corrupting nature of our delusions and self-destructive habits have had no impact whatsoever on our true nature. We need to deal with our conflicting emotions and delusory states of mind because as long as they remain a part of our make-up, any attempt to make something of ourselves will be tainted by those delusions.

There are methods for dealing with ourselves in both the sutric and tantric teachings. In the sutric method, the real emphasis is on taming ourselves, on trying to minimize our physical activities. For example, when we do sitting meditation according to the sutric method, we do not do anything; we just sit still. Physical activity is reduced to the bare minimum. Only breathing is allowed and verbally, we keep silent. There are no prayers that we have to chant, supplications, or pleadings to gods, goddesses, or God. Mentally, we attempt to disengage from all forms of thinking, trying to ensure that we are not caught up in disturbing or discursive thoughts, or being overwhelmed by the conflicting emotions of excessive anger, desire, jealousy, and so on. We aim for a complete reduction of mental, verbal, and physical activities. Even in post-meditation situations, the fundamental practice is to always be aware and attentive, trying to avoid being caught up in the busyness of the physical, mental, and verbal activities of everyday affairs. We try not to feel excessively anxious or become preoccupied by agitated states of mind, including distractions when considering potentially damaging or catastrophic events in the future. We try not to waste our breath by engaging in what, in Buddhism, is often referred to as "chatter." This refers to gossip or idle conversation about inconsequential matters that are of little or no importance and may even cause harm. Once we have uttered whatever it is that we have said, we cannot take it back. Buddhism lists many ills associated with uncontrolled speech. Physically, we also begin to become conscious of the fact that many of our normal activities are harmful and not as neutral as we may have assumed them to be. They in fact cause harm to both ourselves and others. In sutric teachings therefore, the emphasis is on reduction, on minimizing and simplifying. This is why it is difficult to practice according to the sutric method. It is extremely difficult to be vigilant at all times. We cannot remain aware and focused twenty-four hours a day. It is even extremely difficult to remain fully attentive for a short time.

In tantric practice, the emphasis is not on simplifying things. It is not about making everything more elaborate or complex either. However, since we, as human beings, already engage in a variety of physical, verbal, and mental activities, we utilize them instead of trying to control them in any unnatural way. Another point that is emphasized in Tantrism is working with one's natural tendencies. In other words, instead of regarding our wildness as something to tame, we can use it to progress.

When we do tantric meditation, we regularly use *mudras* or hand gestures. There are many different mudras, some of which are extremely complex. Sometimes you have to spend many hours trying to master them. There is one particular tantric practice, for instance, called *Kun druk* in Tibetan, which means, "all seeing." There are many complex mudras in this deity yoga practice. If we wanted to learn extremely complicated movements in dance for example, we would also have to spend a lot of time mastering each movement. The mudras may be similarly complex and refined. Instead of simplifying our activities, the elaborateness of the physical movements is itself used in order to enhance our sense of awareness. If we are sitting quietly, without any movement, our mind may tend to wander more easily than if we had something to do. If we engage in these physical mudras, it keeps our attention. One can also dance in a meditative state; some in the west have called this the "lama dance." Dancing as a god or goddess[2] to manifest the energy or qualities of a particular deity, one experiences and becomes those qualities or energy. Each step that one takes, each movement of the hands, and each gesture reflect the qualities of that divinity.

Verbally, one does not remain silent. One has to use a *sadhana* or ritual text, chanting and making offerings. In order to visualize the deities, one has to chant to invite the deity and their entourage. There is also that element involved. It is not just a simple case of chanting; it can be simple, but it may also be very elaborate. In one particular sadhana, there may be three or four different tunes because often, each segment of a sadhana has a specific tune. Getting to know the tune and trying to get it right requires attention to the voice and the sound that one produces. Of course, all of this is regulated, one cannot just simply do it any way that one wishes or finds comfortable.

In terms of the mind, instead of trying to reduce the mind's discursive thoughts and activities, we can use them as part of our practice. Again, we are not talking about increasing the discursive thoughts, but as they are already present, why not use them in the service of our meditative state? In other words, instead of thinking that they are the enemy of a meditative state, we can utilize discursive thoughts to attain a meditative state. This is achieved by imagining anything from a very simple visualization to an elaborate one. A simple visualization can consist of a single syllable, such as *HUM* or *TAM*. These syllables represent the full divine[3] energy of the respective deity. Some of the visualizations consist of a full *mandala*, that consist of literally hundreds of figures, each having a role to play in the whole display of the divine, all in concert with each other, and all in concordance with a very well-defined, arranged display.

In order to visualize the deities, we generate the appropriate feelings, emotions, and thoughts, and use our imagination to create an inner experience of the deity. All the different activities of the mind are utilized, and we draw on experiences within our own lives. While we may be generating certain appropriate emotions regarding a particular deity, the central figure may be either male or female and the emotions that one generates can depend upon the gender of that central figure. That deity is then surrounded by many other divinities. While we are engaged in this practice of generating the appropriate emotions and utilizing our discursive thoughts and imagination, we are still in a meditative state. That visualization practice of deity yoga is meditation. In this instance, the term "yoga" simply means "integration."

Utilizing whatever is available is the tantric method. Even if your visualization of a deity is unclear or blurred, you can utilize that because you are still in meditation. Whether you can actually visualize something vividly or not depends upon the individual. Some people can and some cannot, but that does not mean that the person who can visualize vividly is going to gain more benefit. The experience that is generated can be the more significant aspect. Some people are also good at holding a tune, while others have problems with it. That, again, is secondary. The most important thing is to remain focused and genuinely try to make use of that opportunity. Just because one's tune does not sound so pleasant does not mean it is going to affect one's meditation in an adverse way. The chanting is designed to activate the psychophysical energy centers (Skt. *chakras*) in your body, through the vibration of sound. It is not only about chanting, it is also about putting yourself into a certain physical state. How you sing and from where you sing produce different physical, emotional, and mental responses. When you first start doing tantric practices, you may find it strange and foreign, however, after a while, you will be able to overcome that. It is all about familiarity.

In that way, there is no notion of simplifying or minimizing our physical, verbal, and mental actions, but rather, it is a matter of utilizing one's body, speech, and mind. In Buddhism, the body, speech, and mind should not be understood as three different entities. They are three different fields of activity that overlap each other. They are not three separate monadic[4] entities, but rather, spheres interacting with each other. One's body, speech, and mind are incorporated into the mandala. They do not operate outside of its sphere. All three become expressions of the same divine mandala.

In terms of our senses, nothing is blocked out or excluded. In the sutric approach, the visual, audial, and nasal senses are generally ignored; we try not to be aware of them or distracted by them, and just concentrate our mind on one object. In Tantrism, on the other hand, visual displays are used for the eyes, nasal objects are used for the nose, and music is played for the ears. Ritual feast, or *tsog* in Tibetan, is consumed for taste; nectar, or *amrita* in Tibetan, is drunk. Different garments are also worn depending upon which tantric practice one is doing. Sometimes one wears a particular hat, headpiece, or at times, a fake wig. You may also wear crowns as well as anklets, bracelets, and necklaces. Many different things like that are employed in order to secure the senses as part of meditation practice.

This is why it is said that tantric practice is easy to practice but hard to understand. The seeming accessibility or facility of the tantric practice can be dangerous. It is easy to think that all these practices are straightforward, but we can fail to properly utilize tantric practices. There is also a difference in the view, as Buddhists would call it, between the exoteric and esoteric approaches. However, the difference in the view is not as great as the difference in the practice. In addition, there is a difference in how the goal, the state of enlightenment, is achieved. All of these differences come from Tantrism's willingness to work with our human condition directly.

According to the sutric approach, attaining the goal is like a fruit with many layers. We must peel away the layers slowly, one after the other, until we eventually reach the inside of the fruit and are able to procure the precious kernel hidden there. The tantric method is not like that. Here, the layers that encase the kernel and the kernel itself are regarded as the same fruit. We are not required to gradually peel away the layers of delusions. We have to develop the skill so we can utilize our delusions, without needing to eliminate them, and they will reveal to us our true nature. The layers of delusions operate as obscuring agents only when we do not have that type of skill. Therefore, once we become familiar with the tantric methods and teachings, we can utilize these obscurations so that our goal is achieved by means of the path itself. In Tantrism, there is no difference between the means and the end itself. The means that we use will reveal the end, which is our true nature.

Our true nature will be attained when there is freedom from all the defilements and freedom from the state of ignorance. Wisdom will arise once the defilements are transformed; they do not need to be eliminated. The point is that by skillfully using what is in the mind, what was defiled is no longer defiled. It is like a very highly trained cook who can prepare a poisonous fish and serve it in a way that one will not get sick. An unskilled cook, on the other hand, may serve good fish and make everyone sick.

Chapter Two

The Sutric Heritage in Tantra and the Clear Light Mind of Bliss

Despite the differences between Sutra and Tantra, it is important to understand how the sutric Mahayana teachings have been appropriated and incorporated into tantric Mahayana.[5] Although there are variations in approach, in tantric Mahayana, one is trying to realize the same as in sutric Mahayana. It is only that exoteric teachings emphasize notions of restraint and renunciation so that one endeavors to engage less in physical and verbal activities and dwell less on discursive thoughts. In the tantric Mahayana or esoteric teachings on the other hand, one utilizes one's body, speech, and mind in their current state to further oneself on the spiritual path. In that way, whatever we engage in physically, verbally, and mentally is transformed. The idea is that we no longer consider what we do as the most significant. It is more a question of the way we do it. Do we engage in something with or without skill? If we are engaged in tantric practices, whatever we do has the potential to be transformed. The tantric understanding of how we do this is founded on the sutric Mahayana teachings.

It seems that in the west, there has been a growing polarization between spirituality and religion, experience and faith, along with a burgeoning of spiritual phenomena. In these contemporary times, all manner of spiritual traditions, techniques, and methods are on offer. However, the emphasis on faith or the religious aspects of spiritual practice have correspondingly become somewhat devalued. Religion, broadly speaking, consists of particular traditions, myths, stories, doctrines, and philosophical and theological teachings, along with techniques that are meant to induce or generate specific spiritual experiences. The myths, story telling, and doctrinal aspects of the many traditions have been devalued because these attributes of religion are supposed to be based on faith. Spirituality, on the other hand, is supposed to be founded in and on experience, and therefore, is regarded by many as more legitimate. Personal experience has been legitimized in the west because it is understood to be more reasonable, rational, and coterminous with a scientific way of thinking. This correlation seems fairly dubious to me.

From the Buddhist point of view, we cannot take the option of privileging personal experience over religious tradition. In the past, it is true that the spiritual aspects of some monotheistic traditions have not been granted the same credibility as dogmas and creeds. As a result, when people discover spirituality, they want to dissociate themselves from the doctrinal aspects of certain religious traditions. As Buddhists, we would have to regard this as risky because we cannot rely on our experiences to explain everything. If we are to believe the Buddhist teachings and take them seriously—a point of issue that is questionable for people who only want to rely on their own experience—we cannot use our own experience as a yardstick. Experience cannot act as the be-all and end-all of our spiritual life.

Our spiritual experiences, as with experiences in life generally, are feeble and open to interpretation. Experiences can be deceptive and fool us into thinking that something is going on when in fact something completely to the contrary is occurring. It is difficult to fully know and understand what we are experiencing without traditional guidelines to follow. This is what is provided by the teachings, including the mythical stories or hagiographies of spiritually realized beings. The doctrinal and philosophical aspects of these teachings guide us by providing information on how to pursue our spiritual path and handle our spiritual experiences. Our spiritual experiences do not occur in a vacuum. We always have to interpret them even though there are possibly no discursive thoughts involved at the time if the experience is non-conceptual. However, if we have an experience, we need to make sense of it and try to understand what it means. We can do this far more effectively by using the conceptual lens that the traditional teachings afford us.

In that way, a real marriage of experience and faith, a merging between our spiritual experiences and the overarching religious framework is needed. Otherwise, all individuals who are on the spiritual path will be inventing their own religious tradition. If we venture into the New Age section of a bookstore, we may find many have a philosophy and religion to offer. Often it can be reported that they do not believe in any specific religious tradition. However, it often appears that they have their own on offer in competition with the more established traditions of the world.

Buddhism has always placed strong emphasis on spirituality and spiritual experiences. It does not matter which tradition of Buddhism we train in, there is always the spiritual component. If we go to Thailand for example, we will be trained in the Theravada tradition of spiritual methods and practices. If we go to Japan, we will be trained in the various Japanese schools of Buddhism, including Zen, which has a very strong spiritual component and the same is true of Tibetan Buddhism. Spirituality has always been emphasized. Even so, we should not overemphasize the spiritual aspect and wrench it from its traditional moorings. By removing the framework, we can easily be at a loss. It *does* matter what Buddha, Nagarjuna,[6] Buddhaghosa,[7] Dogen,[8] and Guru

Padmasambhava[9] said. Without them as our guides, we cannot really follow the Buddhist path or tradition.

The Sutric Mahayana Framework

As mentioned, we have to situate tantric practices within the context of the general sutric Mahayana framework. Sutric Mahayana has two schools, two main lines of spiritual transmission. One emphasizes the notion of what is called "emptiness" and the other emphasizes the notion of "Buddha-nature." Tantrism has incorporated and appropriated both the notion of emptiness and Buddha-nature and brought them together. Generally speaking, "emptiness" simply means that as deluded human beings, everything that we do and experience is governed by ignorance. This state of "fundamental" or "basic" ignorance consists of seeing things in a dualistic fashion. In other words, according to the Mahayana teachings, seeing things dualistically is a mental construct. The binary concepts of subject/object, mind/matter, inner self/external world, including concepts of ignorance/enlightenment, are only mental constructs. Things do not exist in a dualistic fashion. Dualistic notions reinforce the idea that we have of things being separate, self-sufficient, self-existing entities.

According to Buddhism, this is not merely a philosophical view about how things exist. It is not simply a notion from Buddhist ontology.[10] This is a spiritual insight we have to gain in order to transform ourselves. There are many kinds of philosophical insights that we can have, but they do not change us. We do not automatically become transformed, but, according to Buddhism, if we cease to think in a dualistic fashion, we will be transformed. We will not see in the same way ever again. Not thinking of things in a dualistic fashion means seeing them as existing in relationships, not as existing independently. This means not seeing things in terms of subject and object, "perceiver" and "perceived" (Tib. *dzin yul*;

Skt. *grahaya* and *grahayaka*). When we see things dualistically, we think that there is a perceiver here, as a subject, and a perceived object out there, something that is external to the perceiver, something that is "other." According to Buddhism, the perceiver and the perceived are dependent phenomena, as is everything else. So if everything is a dependent phenomenon, everything is empty of inherent existence. This is what emptiness means. From that, we are able to eschew our fixation on things as having some kind of self-sufficient existence. This, in itself, according to Buddhism, can free or liberate us from the distorted ways of thinking we entangle ourselves in.

The more that we think of things as existing independently, self-sufficiently, and of their own accord, the more our concepts will proliferate. This is called *vikalpa* or *prapanca* in Sanskrit, which means "proliferation of concepts." As a result of this, we will begin to think of all kinds of things as existing, even when they have never conventionally existed at all. With an understanding of emptiness however, we begin to learn how to reduce this tendency of the mind to churn out multitudes of discursive thoughts and conceptual categories. These teachings are attributed to Nagarjuna. Even though the Buddha himself gave such teachings, it was Nagarjuna who gave the detailed explanations of what emptiness means. From him we can see that emptiness does not negate empirical reality. In order to illustrate this point, Chandrakirti, one of Nagarjuna's followers, in his *Madhyamakavatara*, said, "I have no dispute with the world; the world disputes with me." This means that emptiness does not imply that nothing exists at all. In order to understand emptiness, we have to have the "middle view." That is, we do not negate empirical reality, on one hand, and do not become fixated on some kind of enduring notion of an absolute, on the other. If we can manage to view things from that perspective, we will realize emptiness. Nagarjuna said if we can do this, not only will our distorted ways of thinking be cured, but also, our conflicting emotions will subside.

According to Nagarjuna, our emotional upheavals arise from our dualistic way of thinking. We think, "I am being harmed," and "I have been treated badly by this person." "This person" is objectified as the ultimate other, while "I" becomes the subject. The same happens in relation to the experience of attachment and attraction: "I am attracted to this person," "I am attached to this person," "I must have this person," and so forth. Through meditation on emptiness and by developing an understanding of the middle view, we will come to understand emptiness and from that, all of our mental disturbances, both cognitive and affective in nature, can subside.

The other stream of teachings that we have inherited from sutric Mahayana relates to Buddha-nature. The beginning of this teaching is traced back to the time of Asanga.[11] Here, the emphasis was put on Buddha-nature, which means that everything that we think exists with some permanency is empty of inherent existence, so it is emptiness. However, as sentient creatures, there is an element in our cognitive nature, which turns toward enlightenment rather than falling under the influence of the ignorance and delusions of mind. There is an element within us, which is not corrupted, which turns toward awakening rather than confusion, bewilderment, and ignorance.

Having learned how to overcome discursive thoughts through developing a greater appreciation of emptiness, our innate nature, which is Buddha-nature, will become more evident and manifest. For even though we have this nature and our delusions have not impacted it, nonetheless, it remains hidden in dormant form. It is only when the discursive thoughts and so forth are dealt with through meditation on emptiness that the obscuring layers of delusions become lifted and start to clear. We begin to have a glimpse of Buddha-nature. This will then start to grow, according to the sutric Mahayana teachings, into full Buddhahood. Through cultivation and the reduction of discursive thoughts and mental agitation, a spark ignites that develops into the full state of enlightenment.

Asanga saw emptiness as important, and it was incorporated into a new system that emphasized the notion of Buddha-nature. The reasoning behind this shift in emphasis was the argument that if we did not have Buddha-nature, how could we become enlightened? If our whole being is saturated with defilements, delusions, and ignorance, how is it possible to experience a state of awakening? Where would the strength to overpower the overwhelming mass of delusions, defilements, obscurations, karmic traces and dispositions, and idiosyncratic traits and habit patterns come from? According to Asanga and his followers, we can overcome them precisely because our innate nature is pure; it has never been corrupted, never fallen under the influence of the greatest weight of delusions.

These two streams of thought have been incorporated and appropriated into the tantric teachings. When we try to understand Tantra and the use of physical yoga, verbal recitation of mantras, and the visualization of deities, they have to be understood with the concepts of emptiness and Buddha-nature in mind.

How then, does one come to an understanding of emptiness in Tantrism? According to the tantric teachings, it is not only through understanding the lack of inherent existence in all things, there is also another method that can lead to this realization. There are other avenues, such as, the practice of deity yoga and the visualization of dieties, dakas and dakinis, gods and goddesses, and so on. Through this, we come to understand emptiness not just from the position of the non-existence of inherent existence, but also from the understanding of non-duality and union.

In Tantrism, the concept of union is of paramount importance. It is not simply a case of seeing oneself and others as lacking in inherent existence; it is about recognizing the union of self and other. In Tantrism, this specifically refers to the union between the self and the deity as the "other"; then the self and the "other" become one. In that way, our dualistic tendencies are gradually eroded. In visualization practices, first there is oneself and then there is the deity as the other. Then the deity enters into oneself and one becomes the deity. You become the deity and the deity becomes you. That is very interesting; it suggests a proficiency in something like "mental gymnastics," something that is quite an achievement. You become the deity, but the deity also becomes you. Then you become inseparable and remain as one.

The deity is also visualized as inseparable from emptiness. These tantric deities are not made of flesh and blood; they are not living, breathing beings, as such. Their being is inseparable from emptiness. From the tantric Buddhist point of view, this is called the "union between appearance and emptiness." One realizes that the deity is constructed and created through one's own mental act of imagination. However, what we draw upon to construct the deity is not something drawn out of nothing. The material for the construction of the deity is drawn from a state of being which is not limited to our conscious, ego-centered mode of operation. In other words, the deities do not have inherent existence; they are not substantially existing beings. Their nature is emptiness, yet at the same time, it is not the case that they have no reality whatsoever because the deities do appear. They have form; they manifest in specific ways. That non-separability of appearance, the form of the deity, and its nature as emptiness, is another way of understanding the relationship between emptiness and the empirical world, according to Tantrism. Therefore, if we become familiar with deity yoga practice, we will understand our relationship with the world in a different way.

With deity yoga practice, we are learning to gain insight into emptiness. Through the union and dissolution of the deity into oneself, when there is nothing but pure presence and no notion of either union or non-union, comes the real tantric meditative experience. Then blissful luminosity is present. This relates to the sutric Mahayana concept of Buddha-nature. We do not use the term Buddha-nature in Tantrism. Rather, we use the terminology of "light" and "bliss." Sometimes it is translated as "clear light," "luminosity," or the "clear light of bliss." The bliss is produced from the experience of union due to the cessation of dualistic thinking, even if it is just for a moment. That blissful experience is not a vague feeling of bliss or an intensely pleasurable experience alone; there is also a sense of light. According to Tantrism, Buddha-nature, our awakened nature according to Mahayana Buddhism, even has a quasi-physical field to it. In other words, we can see it with our "mind's eye," like a quasi-visual apparition.

According to Tantrism, our spiritual experiences are not purely mental; there is a physical basis to our experiences. Our experience of bliss is not just mental bliss, but also a physical bliss, because from the tantric point of view, there is a union of mind and body that also takes place. One does not view mind and body dualistically, saying, "Mind is separate from the body." Often spiritual people have an aversion to the body but according to Tantrism, a spiritual person has to harness and train the body as much as the mind. We can have quasi-visual apparitions precisely because of the mind/body complex. When the mind is in a certain state, there are corresponding physical changes and operations going on. Tantric terminology speaks about psychophysical energy pathways (Skt. *nadi*) and psychophysical energy centers (Skt. *chakras*) and so on, but in modern terms, all kinds of changes are quite possibly happening in the body on a micro scale. In Tantrism, we are talking about a very subtle level of the body.

One will not be in a state of bliss all the time, even if one is an accomplished tantric practitioner. The bliss comes, according to tantric Buddhism, from being able to channel the psychophysical energy (Skt. *prana*) and the life essence (Skt. *bindu*) into the central psychophysical energy pathway. You have bliss as the prana travels up the energy pathway. When it descends downward, you also have the experience of bliss. This is why bliss is experienced in a psychosomatic fashion. It should also be understood that we do not have to be doing tantric yoga practices to have these kinds of experiences. Tantric yoga is only designed to assist us to bring these experiences along. One can have this experience without deliberately doing yogic practice. Through meditation, the psychophysical energy may enter into the central energy pathway and create the experiences of bliss. From the tantric point of view, if one experiences bliss, one can just reside in that without conceptual and other interferences. If one is doing deity yoga practice and there is no experience of bliss, one need not try to manifest it. If one interferes in this way, there will be less experience of bliss and if one is conceptualizing about it, there will be even less.

There are two stages of tantric practice that we try to familiarize ourselves with in deity yoga. The first is the integration of the deity with oneself, in relation to understanding the non-separability of emptiness and appearance. The second is that once the union and dissolution of the deity into oneself has been achieved, all our gross and subtle mental functions become suspended. At this point of deep meditative bliss, one can have the experience of luminosity. In Tantrism, it is said that we experience this in the heart chakra or psychophysical energy center. This is not in the heart *per se*, but in the center of the body parallel to the heart. This is just a brief description; I will explain this further as we go along.

The main point is that Tantrism has incorporated the sutric notions of emptiness and Buddha-nature into its own system, given them a new interpretation, and employed different methods to achieve their realization. In sutric practice, one has to perfect the six *paramitas*[12] or transcendental actions in order to effect the appropriate change. Here, one employs visualization practices that actually require the use of discursive thoughts. As I stated, we do not need to eliminate these thoughts but rather, use them to construct the deities. Having constructed a deity and realized that the deity's nature is emptiness, its appearance becomes inseparable from emptiness; emptiness and its nature are inseparable. Once this deity is conjoined within oneself, it is revealed as blissful luminosity.

In that way, Tantrism has two stages: the first is called the stage of creative-imagination (Tib. *kyerim*) and the second, the stage of completion (Tib. *zogrim*). The first stage is compared to our experiences of birth and the second stage, the process of death. So there is birth, rebirth, and death, or rather, the process of dying. The first stage is called creative-imagination or generation in Tibetan because here, one is constructing more and more elaborate forms of visualization. The second stage involves the dissolution of everything to the point where the mind is brought down to the simplest focal point, wherein lies the luminosity or clear light of bliss.

Because we ordinarily see everything from our normal perception, everything that we experience is called "impure perception" (Tib. *ma pul* or *towa*). We normally perceive everything from our egoistic point of view. By identifying oneself with the deity in Tantrism, one becomes the deity and the deity becomes the practitioner so there is total union. Subsequently, everything that one experiences is transformed because one is seeing things from a non-egoistic point of view. In tantric language, it is said that one sees things from the deity's point of view. We should not misunderstand this. It does not mean that the deity has been brought within us, and thus dwells within the subject so that the subject disappears.[13] The tantric idea of union is quite different. When tantric Buddhists say that we become a particular deity, we are simply realizing that the deity and the qualities attributed to the deity are also aspects of ourselves.

In the tantric tradition, the deities represent various aspects of ourselves. Different deities have different attributes and qualities. In tantric practice, the varieties of deity yogas help us become more aware of and united with all our many qualities. In this way, as we perform the different deity practices, we can continue to discover a greater richness of attributes and qualities within ourselves than we had realized in the past.

So it is not the case that there is a single deity and that we become one with that deity so that they take possession of our psyche and become us to the point that the old individual has ceased to exist. It is more a question of transfiguration and being reborn with greater awareness so that one begins to operate from a higher level. One eventually sees things from a non-egoistic point of view, which then allows one to see everything as "pure perception" (Tib. *tag dang*). The things that we see, smell, taste and touch, it is said, can be experienced with pure perception. The realization of emptiness and Buddha-nature within oneself is achieved through deity yoga practice. Everything that we experience is instigated, not by our own limited ego, but by a more expansive vision of Buddha-nature or the clear light of bliss mind.

Chapter Three
The Practice of Deity Yoga

There is a lot of commonality between Hindu and Buddhist Tantra. Some rituals and practices are almost indistinguishable.[14] However, what makes Buddhist Tantra Buddhist is how practitioners incorporated and appropriated existing tantric traditions and practices into their mainline traditional practices and interpreted them in Buddhist terms. For example, the notion of emptiness (Skt. *shunyata*) is of extreme importance within Buddhist Tantra, because it is a concept that is unique to Buddhism, as are the notions of bodhicitta[15] and Buddha-nature.

Just as Hindu tantras have many divinities, Buddhism has numerous gods and goddesses that are visualized. However, unlike the Hindu tantras, we do not think of the many divinities as existing independently from our minds. This does not mean that these deities are dependent upon an individual's subjective states of consciousness either. Our egoistic perceptions govern our subjective states of consciousness and our self-perceptions are limited to what we are conscious of as a person and our sense of self-identity. When the Buddhist teachings say that the deities exist in the minds of beings, they are not saying that they exist in any particular subjective individual state of consciousness. This is important because the individual state of consciousness that we are normally aware of is only a small aspect of our potentiality. We can transcend self-imposed egocentric limitations to a greater sense of being.

In Buddhism, the deities number into the thousands. They do not have complete independent existence from the mind, but they do have independent existence from the individual states of consciousness of any particular person. The deity is not dependent upon "my" current state of mind nor is it created by that mind. This is important to understand. Deity yoga is practiced to transcend the states of consciousness that we are aware of. In terms of a greater sense of being, we cannot say that the attributes, qualities, and so forth of the deities are drawn from our unconscious states of mind either.

It is said that if you practice, these deities will sometimes appear spontaneously to you. At times, great tantric Buddhist masters have composed a whole new set of practices based on the revelations that they received from their visionary experience of deities. Even though there are many different kinds of deities, we cannot do all of the practices associated with them. We have to do only a few. Even amongst those, there may be a particular deity that we feel some real affinity with and can communicate with. This is known as the "tutelary deity" (Tib. *yidam*) or one's own personal deity. These deities may manifest themselves in dreams and visions. Even without visions, you may suddenly become inspired to write something and it comes out spontaneously, automatically, without having to think about it in terms of what to write. It is just naturally occurring. In tantric Buddhism, we attribute this to the aspect of ourselves manifesting as the deity.

From the tantric Buddhist point of view, we have to judge any experience we may have of the deity spontaneously appearing from the perspective of whether it is self-serving, whether there is some kind of egoistic satisfaction there. If we are thinking about ourselves, saying, "This is me, I'm doing this," and so forth, then obviously, we are not coming from a non-egocentric place. If we are doing, saying, or experiencing certain things without that type of self-fixation, it can be an epiphany, a numinous experience. It is outside our normal states of consciousness, but not outside our own state of being. It is still coming from us in one sense, not completely from outside.

Tantric deities are known as "wisdom deities" or "wisdom gods." "Wisdom deities" mean that they are manifestations of the mind of the clear light of bliss. "Clear light" is wisdom. Even though we are not conscious of these aspects in terms of our subjective states of consciousness, nonetheless, they are part of our own state of being. Within our tantric practices, we may not be completely free of egocentricity, but the demands the ego puts upon our experiences and practices can diminish over time. When the ego is present, we try to make use of it in order to transcend it. That is instead of submitting ourselves to the ego's manipulative tactics of sabotaging.

According to Buddhism, there is an element of implicit or tacit knowing, an element of wisdom present within our minds that is not self-conscious. The deities have their origin in this state thus allowing, assisting, or aiding us in our efforts to rise above our normal states of consciousness or our normal functioning of the egoistic mind. From the Buddhist point of view, ego always operates in a way that frustrates our efforts to find genuine fulfillment, realization, self-realization, or attainment of self-knowledge. Ego is always about self-deception and its activities are always connected with our delusional states of mind.

By assuming the identity of the deity, by inviting the deity into oneself and becoming that deity so that one sees everything from the deity's point of view, whether it is a male or female deity, one can have experiences that are not ego based. The experiences can become more expansive, liberating, freeing, ecstatic, and blissful because by definition, ego functions in a very narrowing and imprisoning fashion.

A male practitioner may visualize himself to be a goddess and a female practitioner may visualize herself to be a god. Alternatively, they may visualize a deity in the same gender, or an androgynous manifestation. The deity may be full of charm and beauty, rather repulsive, ferocious, or wrathful, seeming almost aggressive in its posturing and demeanor. There is a seemingly endless array of distinctive qualities displayed.

People often wonder about the significance of wrathful deities. Divine wrath is an expression of fearlessness, where nothing that we experience within ourselves, in terms of our delusional states of mind, has the ability to harm us. It can be subjugated and overcome. In Tantrism, we speak about different methods of dealing with what we experience: the first is pacification, the second is expansion, the third is overpowering, and the fourth is destruction. When we visualize a wrathful deity, we can imagine the deity actually carrying out these four actions upon all that we find disturbing and painful within our mind.

In deity yoga, one is given the opportunity to assume multiple forms of identity. One is no longer fixated on the notion of saying, "This is me, I am this." Deity yoga practice frees one up to experience in a variety of ways not normally available to us. As the people from the Gelug School of Tibetan Buddhism[16] are fond of saying, we are stuck in our limited perspectives because of this "self-cherishing ego mind." We want to have a well-defined notion of who we are and our sense of self-worth, or lack of self-worth for that matter, depends on this. In that way, deity yoga practice is self-liberating. We are immediately transported to another level of being by becoming that deity. As we become familiar with deity yoga practice, we come to realize that our notion of who we think we are is constructed in the same fashion as the construction of ourselves as the deity. There is no real separation between the two; they are constructed in the same way.

Five Principles of Deity Yoga

We realize ourselves as the deity through identifying with it. From a tantric Buddhist point of view, deity yoga practices only have heuristic[17] value. They are employed only in order to realize our innate clear light of bliss. Clear light of bliss is formless. The forms, attributes, and qualities of the deities that we come to embody are expressions of that formless nature within us. There are five principles of deity yoga to help with this understanding. They are clarity, purity, stability, divine pride, and bliss.

Clarity

When we at first visualize ourselves to be a deity, we do not think of ourselves as that deity. We are still just ourselves. We then visualize the deity in front of us and invite it to merge with us, asking it to take residence within. The deity is absorbed into us and becomes one with us. When this is going on, the deity is visualized as translucent. This is what is meant by clarity, a translucence that is almost like a holographic image. Instead of visualizing the deity as a solid being with flesh and blood, a ghostly figure, or spirit entity, one visualizes the deity as if seeing a rainbow. A rainbow is translucent, iridescent, and transparent, yet full of vivid colors and brilliance. This aspect of clarity is emphasized because if we visualize the deity in this fashion, it will activate the clear light mind of bliss. The clear light of the mind of bliss becomes expressed through the form of the deity.

Purity

Through visualizing all forms of wrathful, peaceful, female, male, and androgynous deities, the so-called "five poisons" are transformed, that is, the five conflicting emotions of excessive anger, desire, jealousy, pride, and ignorance. There are multitudes of traditional deity practices with varying instructions on how to visualize and practice. The deities all have a particular function in transforming impure, base, instinctual, and unschooled psychic tendencies or energies. These energies are rechanneled and thus transformed. There is always a reason for a deity being wrathful, peaceful, visualized in union with a consort, without a consort, or gender specific, and so on. Even the mount upon which the deity stands has specific transformative significance; it could be a horse, buffalo, or something similar. Some deities are adorned with animal heads, each carrying its own unique, symbolic significance. Because of this rechanneling of energies, what is impure and what is pure become equalized with deity yoga practice, without having to renounce or even guard against the very base and unbridled instinctual tendencies within us. By becoming rechanneled and processed, these tendencies are therefore transformed and purified. These are the reasons why deities are sometimes visualized as horrendous and horrible.

If we do this kind of practice, our normal experience of aggression can decrease. We should not associate aggression with strength. Deity yoga practice will probably make us become stronger, less vulnerable, and less fearful individuals. It does not legitimize aggression. Aggression is processed and dealt with through the practice of visualization. From a Buddhist point of view, we do not need to be aggressive to prevent our being taken advantage of, or trampled on, by others. It is far better to be a stronger individual than to be aggressive. Our aggression is rechanneled. Our aggression has hidden or tacit wisdom within it, which we can realize through deity yoga practice. That is why tantric literature states that the five wisdoms and the five poisons are not essentially different. The five poisons have implicit wisdom within. Through the use of these skillful methods, we can release that wisdom and utilize aggression in a different sense.

Stability

Visualization practice is something that we have to construct.

Stability here refers to difficulty in maintaining a stable visualization of the deity in one's mind. As we are not actually visually looking at something or focusing on a sensory object such as sound, we may have difficulty in maintaining the visualization. We build the visualization up from very simple to the more complex fully formed deity. There are specific details regarding each deity's appearance. They may have more than one head, face, multiple arms and legs, et cetera. Even relatively simple visualizations, such as Chenrezig,[18] Manjushri,[19] or Tara,[20] may be difficult to maintain with stability. In this case, we can focus our mind on whatever it is that we are constructing within the visualization at the time—arm, leg, eyes, crown, or implement that the deity may be holding such as a sword, wheel, or cup. As well as focusing the mind on the full deity or an aspect of the deity, one should also experience the attributes that particular deity embodies such as compassion, purification, wisdom, strength, equanimity, and skillful means, et cetera. In this way, the visualization is inclusive of the deity's posture, qualities, and demeanor. It is often said that deities should be visualized with a hint of a smile on their lips, which can assist us to experience them from the perspective of their appearance, demeanor, and essence.

It is also said that we may become drowsy during visualization practices. If we are drowsy and our mind is overcome by torpor and stupor, we are advised to focus more on the upper portions of the deity's body. If we are feeling agitated and our minds are not able to focus, but wander all over the place, thinking about everything except what we are trying to visualize, we are advised to focus on the lower part of the deity's body—how the particular deity is sitting or standing, as there are many variations used in tantric practice. For example, we may focus on which leg is bent and which is outstretched, which direction they point, and so on. What is the deity sitting on? Sometimes, the deity is standing on an individual, elephant, sun, or moon disk. This may be supported by a lotus throne. One should focus on those areas so gradually one can help to stabilize one's mind.

Divine Pride

With divine pride (Tib. *majalo*), we move away from thoughts such as, "I'm just 'me' doing this practice pretending to be the deity." Instead, we need to generate full confidence in our capacity to realize all that the deity represents so that we become the deity—we discover the deity within ourselves. In that sense, we need full conviction in the reality that all of the attributes of the deity are outward manifestations or variegated forms of our inner clear light of bliss. As mentioned, the clear light of bliss, in itself, has no form as such. It is a simple, subtle state of pure cognition. The outward form of this pure cognition is the deity.

In a sense, one needs to develop an intimate relationship with the deity they are visualizing. It is an intimacy based both on love and reverence so that one is able to serve the deity while at the same time acknowledging the deity to be an expression of one's own self, in this case, an expression of the clear light of bliss. It is not an expression of *atman*, or egoistic mind.[21] Gaining full conviction in that is called "divine pride."

With this intimacy, one can have dialogue with the deity, which is a very common practice in Buddhism. It is a form of dialogue with oneself, dialoguing one aspect of oneself with another aspect of oneself. Although the notion of a lower and higher state of being may come to mind, that would be a mistaken interpretation for tantric Buddhism. It is not the journey of an ascending soul, as such, where one is trying to reach some level of divine plenitude. Rather, it is a case of the luminous power of the clear light mind of bliss itself, breaking through, the radiance of which has permeated all aspects of our being including what Buddhists would call our tainted, defiled nature due to our ignorance and defilements. The radiance seeps through, pervading all aspects of our state of being. This occurs through dialoguing, through an exchange between oneself and the deity.

From a tantric Buddhist point of view, at least, this would not be seen as pure fantasy because that deity is not a simple product of our psychological mind. It is a manifestation of our true ultimate state of being, which has become manifest to us in the form of a particular deity. Dialoguing with that deity would guide us to our own self, to self-knowledge, to the realization of the mind of clear light bliss. In that way, according to Buddhism, the clear light of bliss becomes manifest through the various forms of the deities that one interacts with, each form representing aspects of our own original state of being. Once the deity has been conjured up in our mind, so to speak, our deluded states also become transformed due to the deity yoga practice. The brilliance or luminosity of the clear light of bliss breaks through into all aspects of our being. Thus, our deluded states become transformed and there is no longer any separation.

Bliss

Through deity yoga practice, one has been able to effect transfiguration through the invocation and provocation of the archetypal numinous powers of the various forms of deities. As a result, our whole sense of being and how we experience things can become transformed. Jamgon Kongtrul Rinpoche, a greatly respected nineteenth century Tibetan master of both the Kagyu and Nyingma traditions, says in his *Treasury of Knowledge* that when one becomes transformed into the deity and perceives everything from that perspective, when one has transcended the ego perspective and entered into that divine sense of being, everything that one experiences is blissful. What one experiences through one's senses and what one experiences in relation to inner mental states is bliss inducing. Even our normal experiences of anger, excessive desire, and so forth, will produce bliss rather than the suffering, pain, and misery they normally produce.

Normally, our ego manipulates our experiences. When our experiences have been freed from that manipulation, they are no longer contrived. They become spontaneous manifestations of our own authentic state of being. Jamgon Kongtrul Rinpoche says that the basic level of the experience of joy will lead onto the experience of bliss. That experience will lead to the experience of greater bliss, which leads to the experience of ecstasy, and then culminates in the experience of the state of "pure union" (Skt. *sahaja/sahakarin*; Tib. *Lhan cig jad pa*).

As we can see, bliss is graded. These experiences arise from the practice of the two stages of Tantra: the creative-imagination stage and the fulfillment stage. So there are joys, blisses, ecstasies, and so forth associated with the creative-imagination stage practice, and there are corresponding joys, blisses, and ecstasies associated with the fulfillment stage practice, both leading to the realization of sahaja or the state of "pure union."

The practitioner has to keep these five principles in mind when engaging in the tantric practice of deity yoga in order to remind oneself to perceive the deity with a sense of clarity and pure presence. One will then see the deity in relation to purity so that what is impure becomes pure. Even though deity yoga practice makes use of discursive thoughts, they are nonetheless being used to stabilize the mind in the practice; stability has to be achieved. Then one has to have divine pride and not think that this is some kind of simple psychological trick designed to induce particular spiritual experiences. These practices lead to genuine epiphanies of our true and natural state of being. We also need to realize that if we conduct our deity yoga practices properly, due to the pure perception, we can experience bliss. Even things that used to give us pain and discomfort become bliss producing. These are the five main principles that a tantric practitioner has to base their practice on.

Chapter Four
Empowerment and the Vajra Master

To engage in tantric practice, especially Highest Yoga Tantra, we have to receive "empowerments" (Skt. *abisheka*; Tib. *wang kur*). The meaning of the original Sanskrit term "abisheka" is similar to "anointment" or "sprinkling with water." The Tibetan "wang kur" has a different meaning, which is "empowering someone." After the conferment of abishekas or wang kur, the individual is empowered or given permission to perform certain practices that would be denied to others. Both abisheka and wang kur have this connotation of initiation, the initiation of outsiders into a more secret circle of practitioners, in a manner of speaking. This is necessary because almost all of the advanced tantric practices are not available to normal tantric practitioners, even if they happen to be a Tibetan Buddhist monk or nun. If individuals have not received the appropriate abisheka or empowerment, they will not be allowed to participate in the communal ritual practices in retreat situations or advanced individual practices by themselves.

In India, when Mahayana Buddhists began to practice Tantra, they had to almost smuggle the tantric practices into the monasteries. Many of the great tantric masters were also monks, and they kept them secret. As a consequence, no one knew of their practices. Even now, in the Tibetan traditions, we have the notion that certain highly advanced tantric practices must be kept secret. Even people who have been initiated into Highest Yoga Tantra may still not be given the extremely advanced forms of tantric practice unless they have received further appropriate empowerments. This has to occur in relation to the student and the preceptor, who is called *vajracharya* or vajra master in Tantrism, a tantric guru.

All of these notions of secrecy, secret groups, and so forth may not sit well with the modern notion that everything should be open and nothing kept secret. It is argued that if you have something to keep secret, it must be bad. This kind of reasoning begs the question, if what one is doing is good, why should it not be open to everyone? Traditionally, according to Tantrism, this is not possible because as human beings, we are inculcated to think in certain ways. We have fixed, preconceived notions about what is spiritual, what is not spiritual, what is spiritually acceptable, what is not spiritually acceptable, and so on. As a consequence, certain forms of tantric practice may be challenging to the more conventional religious world orientation.

If one has been initiated into the tantric practice, it will make sense. However, for that to occur, one needs to go through many years of training and practice. Even the most advanced forms of tantric practice, the ones that are kept secret, do not actually present as an affront to our normal or rational minds. They are not completely irrational, making nonsense of everything we hold to be normal and acceptable. Nonetheless, certain tantric practices do stretch our normal perceptions of things spiritual. We are so habituated to certain ways of living that when we come to certain spiritual practices, we are not ready. They may be too overwhelming for us to be able to immediately absorb or appropriate. We have to be introduced gradually to these practices, so that as our capacity increases, we become more and more initiated into these advanced forms of tantric practice.

The notion of empowerment is strongly emphasized, because the receiving of empowerments is called the "path of maturation" or "path that enables one to mature" (Tib. *min je kyi lam*). "Min" means "mature," "je" means "that which enables," and "kyi lam" means "path." The empowerments that one receives are designed to aid us in our ability to mature faster. This means that we have the potential to both manifest ourselves as various deities and so forth, as well as to realize our essence of true Buddhahood within. If we do not receive empowerments, these dormant "spiritual seeds," as they are called, are not activated. The empowerments activate these dormant seeds and thus allow us to mature more rapidly on the path.

That is why one has to receive different kinds of empowerments at specified points in the course of one's spiritual development. In other words, higher and higher forms of empowerments are taken. Since the empowerment that the tantric practitioner must receive is so important, they have to receive it from someone who has the authority to bestow it. The would-be tantric initiate is called a *sadhaka*, meaning a practitioner. Those who are quite advanced in tantric practices are referred to as *yogis* or *yoginis*; otherwise they are simply referred to as tantric sadhakas (Tib. *Drubpa po*). A sadhaka is someone who practices a tantric *sadhana* (Tib. *drub thab*), which literally means "method of practice." The sadhaka will realize *siddhis* or "spiritual boons" received from and through engaging in these tantric practices.

The tantric sadhaka has to receive empowerments from someone who has the authority to impart them. This individual must have already received the empowerments that relate to the tantric practice the would-be initiate wishes to practice. It might be the case that an extremely learned and advanced tantric vajracharya, who is in possession of a whole host of tantric teachings, has not received the particular teachings and relevant empowerments related to a sadhana practice in question. In that case, the vajracharya is not qualified to impart that practice. Tantrism can be very strict in this way.

It is said that the qualifications of the vajracharya are extremely important. They must have certain qualities and attributes and the would-be initiate has to search for someone who meets these requirements. It is said that one should not simply take empowerments because somebody happens to be in town and is offering them! We are not talking about that variety of empowerment. That kind of empowerment is made public and the people who receive it do not have to make any real commitment, as such. We are talking about serious tantric practitioners.

If one wants to be a serious tantric practitioner, one has to approach a vajracharya and take the time to get to know them. It is not the case that one simply meets someone who happens to be a great master and in desperation, takes the opportunity to receive an empowerment. The ideal situation would be that the sadhaka actually gets to know the vajracharya and the vajracharya, in turn, gets to know the sadhaka. This is important because there are numerous and varied tantric practices. In tantric literature, the vajracharya's ability to determine which tantric practice would be of most benefit to a particular individual is described as an art. The consequence is that the practice is designed for the particular individual ensuring that they receive maximum benefit from their practice. This can be done only if the vajracharya already has some understanding of the initiate's predilections, personality, and character traits. The vajracharya subsequently knows the particular individual's manifest positive and negative qualities and further, is familiar with the practices designed to deal with the kinds of concerns that person may have.

The student, in turn, has to observe the vajracharya. It is repeatedly emphasized in Tantrism that even an extremely advanced vajracharya may not be suitable for everyone. The initiate has to do their best to see whether a particular vajra master is suitable in terms of their personality, bearing, methods of dealing with their students, and communicating the Dharma, Buddhist teachings.

Of course, the vajracharya must have many qualities, but essentially, they should be highly skilled in everything related to Tantra. In Tantrism, that means skill in many areas. It does not simply mean that the vajracharya has to know the tantric teachings and practices. They also need to know a great deal about tantric rituals, which are particularly complex and subtle. The vajracharya therefore, must have some artistic talents. For instance, they need knowledge in constructing mandalas or creating geometric shapes to sanctify the ground so that an initiation can take place. If a ritual is to be performed, they must know how that ritual is executed.

Not all tantric rituals are performed in the same way. Each tantric deity has its own sadhana, which has a set of rituals performed in a specific way. This may sound as if it is an unnecessarily complicated affair, but from the tantric Buddhist point of view, this knowledge is extremely important. The rituals themselves are not simply insignificant rites that are being performed; the rituals themselves carry power. The difference between knowing and not knowing the relevant tantric literature might mean that whatever tantric function one is trying to create will either flourish or suffer setbacks and encounter obstacles. Many of these tantric rituals have two functions: one is to expel the negative forces from the designated area and the other, to protect that area so that these negative forces do not return and cause upsets. For instance, if you want to construct a Buddhist reliquary, rituals of this nature have to be performed. If one is taking an empowerment, these kinds of rituals also have to be implemented.

It is important to keep this in mind, because according to Tantrism, making a domain sacred and keeping it untarnished and uncontaminated by evil influences is extremely important. It is the same when one is doing a tantric sadhana practice. You first expel or eliminate all the obstacles, the evil, negative forces, and then you try to create a dome of protection. You then proceed with the practice in the safety of this so-called "vajra dome."

The vajra master has to be very skilled with this process. They also have to be skilled with the actual practices, knowing everything about the outer and inner tantras. The "outer" tantras are the lower tantras and therefore more accessible to the public. The "inner" tantras are the higher tantras and not so accessible to the public or even to some initiates. Some of the inner tantras are not even available to ordained, celibate monastics.

The vajracharya has to be skilled in these areas as well as be spiritually advanced. However, this does not mean that the vajracharya is beyond any fault or defect whatsoever. In tantric teachings, they insist on this point. It does not mean that when we find a vajracharya, they must be perfect or beyond reproach. It has been said by Jamgon Kongtrul Rinpoche, Dakpo Tashi Namgyal,[22] and other masters, that this simply means that the vajracharya has more positive than negative qualities. In other words, the vajracharya has to have more redeeming qualities than repulsive or demeaning ones. According to the great masters themselves, one of the qualities that a teacher must have is bodhichitta or loving-kindness. This does not mean "loving-kindness" in the normal secular sense but rather refers to "loving-kindness" in the Mahayana Buddhist sense of caring for the welfare of everyone; someone who is deeply moved by others. What others are experiencing is very important to the vajra master. They not only show loving-kindness toward those they favor, but also care for everyone.

First, the vajracharya has to find a tantric initiate who has certain qualities. Again, of course, the student will not be perfect, they may have a variety of faults, but to be acceptable, it is said that the student must be someone who is inquisitive and who wishes to learn. The point here is that some may not have real eagerness to learn; they may want to be initiated into tantric practices for wrong or selfish reasons.

The second quality that is required of a student is to not be arrogant or self-centered, but to have a sense of humility. In fact, these two qualities go together. If there is a sense of humility, there is a willingness to learn. If one has greater arrogance, then there is less willingness to learn, or if such a person is learning, it is more likely that they will argue with their teacher. So arrogance, self-centeredness, or pride should be lessened. Not to have them at all is most likely impossible, but there needs to be a sense of humility and willingness to learn.

The other quality that is often mentioned is kindness. Just like the vajra master having this notion of loving-kindness toward all, the student generally needs to have a kindly disposition, instead of a very uptight, naturally aggressive one. If one has these qualities, one can approach a teacher.

In Tantrism, the vajracharya does not normally tell the student which practice they should be doing. It is up to the student to approach the vajracharya and request specific practices. In Tantrism, it is said that one has to make this request again and again. It is part of the traditional approach that most vajracharyas will deny the request three times. It is said that the student must approach the teacher and request the relevant practice that one wants to engage in and to receive the required empowerment at least three times.

Of course, often the request may have to be made more than three times, as was the case with Milarepa.[23] Every time we make that request however, our resolve becomes stronger and our determination to do the practice becomes strengthened. If our resolve was not so strong to begin with, being denied after our first request may prompt us to proceed no further. It would have been appropriate for the vajracharya to refuse that entreaty, precisely because real resolve and determination were not present. If we persist with our request, second, third, fourth, or fifth request, our determination grows stronger. This is what happened with Milarepa. Every time Marpa refused him empowerments, his resolve grew stronger rather than weaker.

"Three times" is mentioned, but it is said, "at least three times." Basically, it is about showing one's seriousness. When it says "three times," that does not mean that you ask the vajracharya once in the morning, go back in the afternoon, and then ask again in the evening. One has to give some time before making the next request. This is true not only in tantric Buddhism but also in Zen Buddhism. For example, a student may go to the Zen teacher, be refused, and then spend the whole night outside the roshi's[24] room in the freezing cold; enduring other difficulties, and still be refused again and again until deemed ready.

If we go through this process, as soon as we have made that resolve or determination, something in us, mentally, psychologically, and spiritually, has already been set in motion. It all depends on our attitude. If we are causal about it, we will not get much benefit, but if we are sincere and grateful, receiving these teachings, empowerments, and practices with a committed, clear, and positive mental attitude, then we receive many benefits.

In this way, the rapport between the teacher and student is established and they begin to develop lines of communication. This implies that the communication is personal and unique. In terms of a student's tantric practice, the vajracharya does not respond in the same way to everyone. There are many stories where the same master has given different practices to different students who may all have been practicing under that master at the same time. This is common even to this day. Many students go to their vajracharya to receive empowerments, but each student is communicated with differently and in a unique fashion.

In that way, teacher and student should remain in contact. This does not mean physically necessarily, but there should be contact over a long period of time to continue the connection and to know one another better. The tantric literature says that it usually takes about twelve years for the teacher and student to get to a level where they are both completely at ease. It takes that long for genuine rapport or rapprochement to develop. After this prolonged period of "checking each other out," the teacher and student get to a level where there is a real meeting of minds. Of course, the teacher is there to awaken the clear light of bliss in the student, which is inseparable from the clear light of bliss of the vajracharya, which in turn, is inseparable from the clear light of bliss in the essence of Buddhahood itself.

For these reasons, the notion of vajracharya is considered to be extremely important. The relationship is such that it takes a long time to grow, mature, and flower and for the tantric sadhaka to receive all the relevant instructions and empowerments. In this way, the sadhaka becomes a qualified yogi or yogini and even, possibly at a later point, a vajracharya. This extensive time period is necessary because it takes a long time for the student's mind to expand enough that they will be able to fathom and comprehend more and more advanced levels of teachings. What may be received with incredulousness if introduced prematurely, will be comprehended if imparted at the appropriate time. Buddhism says that when the circumstance of auspicious coincidence is present, the student's mind will expand until they are able to receive and understand the depth of increasingly advanced and profound teachings.

If one's mind is able to develop, all of these advanced levels of Tantra will make sense. However if our mind is not so advanced, these teachings will not only make no sense, they will also be seen as ludicrous and completely aberrant. Some individuals have viewed tantric teachings in that way. If one's level of understanding has increased, it will make sense. As it is said in the Buddhist teachings, what does not make sense to a child, will make sense to an adolescent and what does not make sense to an adolescent, will make sense to an adult. If we try to explain everything that an adult understands to a child or adolescent, they will not be able to comprehend it. Their mind will not be equipped to take it in.

It is similar with tantric teachings. This is why Tantrism has a hierarchy in terms of secrecy. Tantrism contains things that are quite secret, more secret, extremely secret, and those rarely shared. Some secrets are kept from almost everyone. Very few Tibetan masters may know some of them. Even having the texts and knowing them is of no use because they are written in coded language. If you do not know how to decode the language, you are at a loss. There are many tantric texts of that nature; texts that mean something completely different from what they say because what is written has nothing to do with what is actually meant. It is not simply a case of the texts requiring philosophical interpretation, that their import is somewhat ambiguous and could be interpreted on a number of different levels or contain the possibility of multiple readings. There is actually no relationship between the words and the meaning in many instances. Only highly advanced, learned masters would understand some of these interpretations. This is why Tantrism is very secretive and esoteric and also why commitment is emphasized so much.

The commitment is important because we believe in the importance of progress and attainment because of the belief in rebirth. The tantric reasoning is that if we have been taking rebirth for such a long time, we need to ensure progress on the spiritual path. Taking a number of years to gain a profound understanding of ourselves, relatively speaking, is not long. The tantric path is called the "short path" (Tib. *Nyur lam*), but it still requires a sustained commitment. With that sustained commitment, one gradually becomes a fully qualified tantric practitioner. That can only happen if we are in the good hands of a competent and able vajracharya.

The qualities of the vajracharya have to be based on qualities that are mentioned in the sutric or exoteric Mahayana teachings. In exoteric Mahayana, it is said that any Mahayana teacher must have the qualities of a *ke tsun zang sum* in Tibetan. "Ke" means that the teacher has to be "well-versed in Buddhist theories and practices," "tsun" means the teacher must have "pleasant manners," meaning that they are not too rough, tending toward the gentle side, and "zang" means "kindly disposed" or "kind-hearted." These are the three sets of qualities that a Mahayana teacher generally must have.

That teacher needs to have three additional qualities, called "*Chad Tsod Tsom sum*" in Tibetan. These are actually an extension of the first quality of being "well-versed in Buddhist theories and practices." "Chad" means "exposition," someone who is not only extremely well informed about various matters related to Buddhism, but who is also highly skilled in communicating that to others, a skilled teacher. "Tsod" means "someone who can offer good reasons for making certain claims regarding Buddhist spiritual theories and practices," and "someone who can debate well and present a good case through being skilled with the use of logic and reasoning." "Tsom" means "composition," someone who can explain things well in written form.

These are qualities that, according to Mahayana Buddhism, all Mahayana Buddhist teachers must have. Mahayana students must also aspire toward developing these qualities and attributes. If a teacher has some or all of these qualities, this will rub off onto the students and the students will in turn, start to develop the qualities as well. The tantric qualities that I mentioned have to be added on to these. The tantric master should have extensive knowledge of all aspects of general Buddhist theories and practices, and of both

Buddhist sutric and tantric teachings. If that individual is not informed, they will not be a very good vajracharya.

Chapter Five

The Preparatory Arrangements
for the Empowerment

Before we can discuss the actual tantric empowerments, we have to discuss their preparatory arrangements. When we take an empowerment, it has to be a significant event in one's life. We cannot simply go to a vajracharya, ask for an empowerment, and have everything done in a haphazard, hasty fashion without worthy attention and buildup. It is said that one must have the feeling that something of major significance is going to happen when one takes an empowerment.

The taking of an empowerment is different to the initiation rites of passage for young adults that are conducted the world over. However, it is similar to this to the extent that those rites are seen as extremely important for the individuals who are being initiated. It is a turning point in their lives; it is an event. Similarly, when an individual takes a tantric empowerment, they are ushered into a whole new and sacred world. One has to have the feeling that one is stepping into a sacred environment, that something old is being left behind, and that a whole new world is opening up. These so-called "preparatory arrangements" are made in order to bring that sense of event and real occasion to the experience of empowerment.

Creating the Right Environment

First, one has to create the right environment. Instead of simply casually conferring the empowerment to the individual who has made the request in an arbitrary environment, the environment should be transformed into a sacred and encircled space. This is achieved through creating a mandala. There are three different types of mandala that are suitable.

The best way of creating the appropriate atmosphere for this occasion is to construct the mandala with the use of colored sand (Tib. *dul tson*). "Dul" means "sand grains" and "tson" means "colored." These colors have symbolic meaning attached to them. It is not a matter of finding some colored sands and simply scattering them on the ground; they represent various forms of the wisdom energy of the "five Buddha families."[25] Alternatively, the mandala can be drawn on a piece of cloth and laid out on the ground. If, however, none of these materials are at hand, or are extremely hard to obtain for some reason, one's own body or mind can be used as the mandala through an act of imagination. This is only if the other two items are unavailable. If they are, then one must insist upon using them to create the mandala. These first two mandalas, the mystic circle of drawing on the ground with colored sand and the mandala painted on a piece of cloth, are known as "contrived mandala," while the body and mind mandalas are "non-contrived mandala."

If we have the necessary resources to create the mandala with colored sand, we conduct this process in three stages. This would normally done by an appropriately qualified monastic or lama:

1. The first is in relation to geomancy, about the importance of determining and choosing the right place for the empowerment to take place.

2. The second concerns asking the earth deity for the use of the space instead of simply invading the space, and setting things up and proceeding with the various rituals. As part of this, one has to bless the vases that will be part of the initiation practice,

arrange them properly on the shrine, and so on.

3. The third is about the initiates themselves, as they have to be consecrated and made ready recipients for the empowerment to take place.

This is then followed by the actual conferment of the empowerment.

Geomancy

The direction of the place where the empowerment is to be located needs to be considered—north, south, east, or west? Having determined where it is to be located, ritual practices would be required to transform the area into an appropriate place for the ritual performance. The quality of the earth must also be checked in terms of color. It has to be determined whether it is red, black, sandy, or rocky. Other characteristics the land has, for example, in terms of shape and form, have to also be determined. This includes looking at the location in relation to the vicinity of water and other characteristics. Having investigated all of this under the direction of the vajracharya, the vajra master will then decide on the precise place to conduct the ritual.

Requesting Permission from the Earth Goddess

Permission from the earth deity or goddess then has to be requested before the empowerment can proceed. There are four steps in this process. The first one is a request for the area to be used for this purpose. The second is the purification of that area. The third is taking possession or occupation of that space. The fourth and final step is the protection of that space.

Step One

If there are any local spirits or beings associated with the water, trees, creeks, and so on, permission is sought from them to proceed with the empowerment.

Step Two

After that, the earth has to be dug and one observes to see if any crawly beings come out. These are called "beings that move on their belly," which include snakes and similar creatures. Snakes, of course, in Indian mythology, are associated with subterranean beings (Skt. *nagas*; Tib. *klu*). This is part of the purification of the ground ritual. If any crawly things come out, the vajracharya will have a host of knowledge about what that means. Certain creatures will signify one thing and other creatures will denote something else. The vajracharya will also have the relevant information in terms of something negative emerging and will be able to nullify the evil influences that may have been stirred up by digging into the ground. Whatever dirt has been dug up is piled into a small heap and the vajracharya will bring all manner of consecrated substances to sprinkle over it. They will also utter mantras and use the power of meditative concentration in order to purify that piece of earth. The area is subsequently completely expunged of evil influences through these means.

Step Three

The third step is called "taking occupation of that space," which is done by visualizing the palatial mansion in the mandala of the relevant deity. Once that has been done, whichever deity is involved, whether it be Chakrasamvara, Hevajra, Guhyasamaja, or any of the Highest Yoga Tantra deities, is invoked and invited to that spot and requested to take a seat in the imagined palatial mansion. The initiate then makes a request for the empowerment (Skt. *abisheka.*) The vajracharya will then lift the mandala into the air and, through their meditative concentration, generate the divine pride of the particular deity in question. With that experience of divine pride, the vajracharya, while reciting tantric or mantric formulas, forces all of the negative elements of that cordoned off area to exit. The vajracharya expels all of these negative forces holding the bell in the left hand and waving the vajra in the right hand. By waving the vajra around and reciting the formulas in a ferocious manner, the vajracharya drives out all the negative forces from this consecrated area. This is called the "ritual of vajra sweeping." All of the beings that are not wanted are made to leave through this ritual.

Step Four

The final step in creating this sacred ground is the protection of the area. Here, the designated area is completely encircled and cordoned off by this "vajra dome" so that no evil force can penetrate from the outside and cause disruptions while the ceremony is taking place. Then, those recalcitrant beings that have still refused to leave the area are mercifully nailed to the ground! Of course, this is symbolic not literal because in Buddhism, killing sentient creatures is absolutely forbidden, be they human or spirits. This is a symbolic act of protection. As we tend to think in terms of being disturbed by negative forces and evil influences, rituals of this kind are effective. Having done this, one has to ensure that no evil forces will return and the appropriate ritual formulas are also recited. However, if the empowerment is going to be conducted in a place where similar practices have been conducted in the past, these preliminary rituals are unnecessary.[26]

Once the ground has been cleared of all evil influences, consecrated, transformed, and made into a sacred area, the second part in the ritual is performed. This involves making an arrangement to invite the deities and placing them into the mandala. This has to be done by visualizing the mandala and the deities, inviting them, and then placing them in the mandala. While doing this, one also has to draw a demarcation line around the sacred space, which is done by drawing a line. One has to draw the line with a multicolored string. What the string is made from, its length, and so forth, also have to be precisely monitored, as there are specified measurements that have to be kept in mind. This drawn line is done around the sacred area within which the central divinity now resides. While doing this, there are other ritual formulas that one has to do, such as making offerings and requesting empowerments from the deities.

The ritual vases are then positioned in the appropriate places and consecrated. We also have to look at what variety of vase is to be used for the specific empowerment. How many ritual vases are needed? What sort of characteristics do these vases need? What kind of consecrated substances should be put inside the vases? What sort of ribbons should be put around the necks and tops of the vases? How should one adorn the opening of the vases, such as with *kusha* grass or peacock feathers? Again, one has to visualize that the deities one is to be initiated into are inside the vases. These deities are known as "the deities of commitment" (Skt. *samayasattva*). Then one needs to do more offerings, supplications, recitation of mantras, and so on.

Consecration of the Initiates

Once the vases are properly arranged and consecrated, deities are invited into the vases where appropriate offerings have been made and the would-be initiates then have to be called and gathered into an orderly group. The vajracharya has to then look at the personality characteristics of each of the students, what they are like, and how many of them there are. They are then seated and sprinkled with water, which is a form of purification. Following this, the would-be initiates make a mandala offering.

Once the initiates have settled on the ground, they have to generate strong motivation to receive the empowerment. They need to build up their sense of expectancy, harden their resolve, make additional supplications, and recite mantras so that the empowerments will be granted. It is essential that a strongly generated sense of motivation to receive the empowerment is present.

In order for the initiates to be fit to become future *tantrikas* or tantric practitioners, the vajracharya blesses their three centers, the crown, throat, and heart center. In order to determine how these would-be tantrikas will fare with their practices, so-called "tooth sticks" are thrown. Indian people use these to clean their teeth in the morning. According to Tantrism, there are signs for everything, including where something lands when you throw it. When a certain kind of atmosphere and environment is created, where and how something lands becomes significant.

In order to signify the verbal impurities of the initiates who are being purified, they are given a scoop of water to drink from their palm. In order to prevent the newly initiated practitioners from having disturbing dreams that night, they are given kusha grass to put under their mattress or pillow. Each person is also presented with a protection cord so that they do not encounter obstacles of any kind. This is followed by a short discourse in order to uplift the spirits of the initiates and make them feel joyous. The dreams they have that night are also interpreted in order to try to decipher their meaning.

The Preparation for the Actual Empowerment

The procedure for drawing the line has to be repeated one more time. Two lines are drawn: the first one is called a "karmic line" and the second is called a "wisdom line." Again, one has to be very specific about the color and length of the string. These lines are drawn in keeping with the seating arrangements or the movement of the footsteps of the initiates, so that they encircle that whole area. One also has to put the appropriate vases on display and further offerings are made. The deity that one is to be initiated into has to be visualized in front of oneself. That visualized deity then becomes absorbed into the colored sand mandala or the mandala painted on a cloth and manifests as the wisdom deity. At this point, further offerings and supplications must be made. Subsequently, the deity has to be visualized inside the main vase and one recites the seed syllable of that deity. This is followed by offerings of small tormas or stylized food offerings to spirits, in this case, not to the deities.

The vajracharya has to receive these empowerments and enter into the mandala so that they become empowered to impart the abisheka to the would-be initiates. The vajracharya then manifests themselves as that deity. Without separating themselves from that deity, they make the preparations for the conferment of the empowerment to the initiates.

That concludes the preparatory arrangements for receiving the empowerment.

Chapter Six
The Four Empowerments

Having found a tantric vajracharya and made the request for the relevant tantric empowerments, the preparatory practices have to be observed. The above description of the preparatory practices was in relation to the full elaborate ritual version. It has been made clear in tantric texts that if, due to circumstances, time restrictions, place, or the unavailability of relevant resources, empowerments can be given mainly through the use of imagination. It is not necessary to sanctify the ground and place the empowerment is to be received and bestowed. However brief it is, nonetheless, some preliminary practice must precede the actual conferment of the empowerment. These preparatory practices are important for creating an atmosphere of celebration and expectancy, for turning the whole event into a true turning point in one's spiritual life and giving a real sense of entering into the very sacred world of the deity mandala.

After going through the various stages of the preparatory practices, one receives the actual tantric empowerments themselves. The empowerment has two functions: the first is that the initiate is purified and anointed and the second is that the initiate is transformed into a sacred individual. The Tibetan word for that is "wang kur," which literally means "bestower of power." "Wang" means "power" and "kur" means "bestow." The individual becomes empowered through being received into, or permitted to enter, the sacred mandala.

There are four types of empowerments, which are bestowed in a particular order. In other words, the way in which the four empowerments are listed is not arbitrary. They are listed in the same order that they are to be conferred. The order also signifies a greater and greater secrecy and each one is said to be more esoteric or potent in nature. The first empowerment is the most basic and is connected with the physical plane or realm. Therefore, it relates to our physical aspects. It is the most elaborate and exoteric, which is often also called the "external empowerment." The last three are known as "internal empowerments," because they are more esoteric in nature, each one possessing increasing potency. The more esoteric ones become increasingly less elaborate. The last empowerment is the least elaborate of all, with hardly anything of physical symbolic nature being conveyed or enacted. It is subtle, imperceptible. The first empowerment is called the "vase empowerment," the second is called the "secret empowerment," the third is called the "wisdom-knowledge empowerment," and the last is called the "empowerment of logos" or the "empowerment of word."

Vase Empowerment

The first empowerment is actually a set of empowerments that are collectively known as the "vase empowerment." This group of empowerments is divided into two types of empowerment sets: the first set is known as the "empowerment of the initiates," which consists of five separate empowerments and the second set is known as the "empowerment of the vajracharya," which consists of nine separate empowerments.

Empowerment of the Initiates

The first empowerment in this set is the "water empowerment." Here, water is poured out of the vase and offered to the initiates to symbolize the purification of the defilements and obscurations of ignorance. Next comes the "crown empowerment," which is given in order to find out one's nature through awakening one's affinity with the deity of a particular Buddha family. There are five Buddha families, which transform the five poisons.[27] Each person is said to have a particular affinity with one of the families. This is followed by the "vajra empowerment." Here a vajra is placed on top of the initiate's head, symbolizing that they will develop the wisdom that is inseparable from "reality as such" or all-encompassing of mind and phenomena.[28] Next, a bell is sounded in order to realize both the non-separability of emptiness and compassion and the very nature of things with the arousal of wisdom. This is the "bell empowerment." In order to receive the real sense of becoming an awakened Buddha in the future and to become renowned as a Buddha in the future, one is given the "name empowerment." These are the five empowerments that constitute the "empowerment of the initiates": water, crown, vajra, bell, and name.

By receiving these five empowerments, the five poisons become transformed into five wisdoms and the five psychophysical constituents of body, feeling, perception, karmic volition, and consciousness become transformed into the five wisdoms of the five Buddha families. Books on Tantra often refer to the five Buddha families as the five "dhyani Buddhas," but there is in reality, no mention of the word "dhyani" in the tantric texts. They are simply referred to as Buddha families. In any case, the seed of the five Buddha families is planted at this point, from having received the five components of the empowerment of the initiates.

Empowerment of the Vajracharya

A series of empowerments known as the "empowerments of the vajracharya" are also given in conjunction with that. These empowerments are aimed at the realization of the wisdom of all buddhas. First, one is given the "empowerment of vajra" in order to bind one to that commitment. One is given the "empowerment of bell" in order to realize that everything that exists has no inherent nature and to bind one to that commitment. One is given the "empowerment of mudra" to not be separated from the personal deity one has taken on binding oneself to that commitment. One is then given the "empowerment of water" in order to realize the purity of one's mind through Vajrasattva,[29] who is the representation of one's own nature of the mind, by symbolically purifying all of one's defilements. One is given the "empowerment of instruction" in order to realize the nature of all things as dependently arising.[30] One is given the "empowerment of mantra" in order to become proficient with the recitation of mantras and so forth.

At this point, in order to symbolize the lifting of the veils of ignorance, the initiate's eyes are covered with a blindfold. It is then lifted to symbolize the lifting of ignorance. Alternatively, one will be given ointment, in order to symbolize the curing of a type of blindness. One is then given the "empowerment of mirror" by being shown a mirror in order to illustrate that everything that exists in the world is inseparable from one's own nature, that everything one sees is comparable to a reflection in a mirror. One is given the "empowerment of bow and arrow" in order to signify the defeat of the four evil powers (Skt. *maras*): the evil of conflicting emotions, death, egoism, and craving and excessive desire. In order for the initiate to be successful and proficient with their deity yoga practice, permission is given for them to engage in the relevant practices. Then, the "empowerment of tantric meditation" is given in order to realize the five wisdoms, not to become separated from bodhicitta, the apprehension of enlightenment, and to become proficient with the practices of tantric yoga. Prophecies will be uttered at this point to signify that the initiate will become a greatly realized being in the future. One is then given the "empowerment of encouragement" so that one has the courage to persist with and successfully accomplish all of the tantric practices.

These empowerments, which are collectively known as the "empowerments of the vajracharya," are given in order to ensure that the initiate will not relapse, suffer setbacks with their practices, nor encounter obstacles. These are the nine empowerments that constitute the "empowerments of the vajracharya": the empowerment of vajra, bell, gesture, water, instruction, mirror, bow and arrow, tantric meditation, and encouragement. Both of these two empowerments, the empowerment of the initiate and the empowerment of the vajracharya are collectively known as the "vase empowerment." The physical empowerments are given collectively, the "empowerment of the initiate" and subsequently the "empowerment of the vajracharya." This concludes the bestowal of the vase empowerment.

Secret Empowerment

It is difficult to get into the details of the "secret empowerment" unless you have been initiated into the practice. It would subsequently be explained more fully. Generally speaking, the "secret empowerment" consists of visualizing one's vajracharya in the form of the deity that one is going to be initiated into. One visualizes them in the union of embrace. Great bliss is generated from this union and nectar (Skt. *amrita*; Tib. *dutsi*) flows down from this great bliss and enters the central energy pathway of the initiate's body. This nectar enters into and unlocks various points in the body that are normally referred to as "knots" in tantric literature. As this nectar flows into the initiate and travels through their body, it induces the experience of bliss.

Normally, due to not being proficient with our meditational practices and unfamiliar with how the psychophysical energies in the body work, we have various knots in our psychophysical energy pathways. These psychophysical energy or pranic pathways are like networks that crisscross at different points of the body, such as the crown, throat, heart, and just below the navel, and become entangled at different points. According to tantric teachings, this is why we get so worked up emotionally and become so confused and swayed by what is happening in our mind. When these so-called "knots" become untangled, we experience bliss.

This is called the "secret empowerment." At this point, in order to symbolize the experience of bliss during the empowerment, certain nectars and other purified substances may be given to the initiate. They are given in order to symbolize this inducement of bliss. The experience of bliss particularly affects the psychophysical energy center of the heart, which allows the individual to realize what is called in Tantrism, "illusory body yoga." The essence of the "secret empowerment" is the tasting of "bodhicitta," which is the nectar. In tantric terminology, "bodhicitta" does not mean "enlightened heart" as it does in the sutric teachings. Rather, it means the nectar that has been produced from the bliss of union. The physical substance, the nectar is also called "relative bodhicitta" in tantric terminology, which simply refers to the physical substance of the nectar.

While the "vase empowerment" focuses on the physical body as the object of empowerment, the "secret empowerment" concentrates on the vocal center as the object. In this case, it is the defilements associated with one's speech that become purified. In the tantric context, speech has a broader connotation than what is normally meant by speech. In other words, speech is not only the articulated sounds we produce, there are other forms of communication that emanate from our being, or speech center, that are also referred to as speech. For instance, in Tantrism, our psychophysical energy pathways are also adorned with various aspects of speech functions. The "secret empowerment" purifies all of one's verbal defilements. The "vase empowerment" is planted on the physical level, so its seed matures into the "physical aspect of

Buddha's being" or *nirmanakaya*. The "secret empowerment" focuses on the verbal level, so its seed matures into the realization of the "communicative aspect of Buddha's being" or *samboghakaya*. With the "vase empowerment" then, one realizes "vajra body" and with the "secret empowerment," one realizes "vajra speech."

Wisdom-Knowledge Empowerment

The third empowerment is given in order to realize the "bliss of co-emergence" or the "bliss of union." When one receives this empowerment, one is allowed to engage in practices that are primarily designed to produce the highest level of ecstasy, called the "ecstasy of union." This is the highest type of union, but it is not "union" in the ordinary sense of the word. It signifies the state of non-duality. There are other, lesser ecstasies that one must work with first to bring about this ecstasy of non-duality. These other kinds of ecstasies come from the experience of union, where one induces these blissful experiences through visualizing deities in union or experiencing normal sexual union. There are three kinds of blisses, from mild forms, to more intense ones. As one gradually becomes more proficient and familiar with the practices, these experiences of bliss lead to the realization of the highest bliss, which is the "bliss of non-dual blissful wisdom" (Tib. *lhan chig yeshe*).

The third empowerment initiates the individual into what you might call the "technology of ecstasy." In Tibetan, "trul khor" literally means "technology." This technology is in relation to how to make use of one's psychophysical energy pathways and energy, and how to work with the psychophysical energy centers. It is the psychophysical energy that activates the mystic heat in the abdominal area. The heat rises upward and causes the melting of the "bodhicitta" in the psychophysical energy center of bliss. This then descends downward.

Celibate practitioners who receive the third empowerment do this practice by visualizing the male and female deities in union, not by practicing union themselves. This has the same result of producing ecstasy and the flow of nectar. Whether one is celibate or non-celibate, practicing sexual union or visualizing male and female deities in union, the result is that mystic heat is generated. The mystic heat rises upward and melts the nectar at the crown center, which then descends downward. The rising of the mystic heat produces four different kinds of joys and the descending of the nectar produces four different kinds of blisses.

In Tantrism, this nectar is referred to as "bodhicitta." "Bodhicitta" literally means "heart of enlightenment," but as I mentioned, in the tantric context, it is used to refer to nectar. The crown center is called the "psychophysical energy center of bliss," the psychophysical energy that ascends with the mystic heat is called "ye bab," and the descending nectar is called "ne bab" in Tibetan, which literally means "rising upward" and "descending downward" respectively. Both of these movements produce the corresponding states of bliss and ecstasy.

In this tantric practice of union, the idea is not to experience sexual orgasm every time. Rather, the tantric practitioner reverses that experience and drives it upward at the last moment in order to experience the four types of bliss. When it descends downward again, the person again tries to control it and reverse it upward. It is sometimes said in Tantrism that someone who is engaged in the practice of sexual union is actually celibate if they have mastered that technique. This kind of practice is not pursued in order to improve one's sex life but rather to transform it so one is able to gain spiritual transcendence.

In this way, the third empowerment empowers the individual to practice the deity yoga that requires union, or one is empowered to practice union with an actual consort.[31] According to Tantricism, we have both male and female elements within us. Through deity yoga practice, even deity yoga union practice, we can gain integration of the feminine and masculine within. According to Tantrism, all our problems come from not having integration. If there is integration or coincidence of our polarities, of the different parts within us, we will be less in conflict with others. In tantric Buddhism, the internal mandala is seen as a microcosm mandala and the external world as a macrocosm mandala. It is also said that we should view the whole universe as a mandala.

Empowerment of Logos or Word

The fourth empowerment is the empowerment of logos or word. This basically means introducing the practitioner to their natural state of the mind and showing that this natural state is no different to that of the mind of an enlightened being. This is the realization of "Mahamudrahood." By receiving the fourth empowerment, one is planted with the seed of realization of Mahamudra, the nature of the mind.

The third empowerment uses the mind as the object in order to transform all of the mental defilements and one realizes *dharmakaya*, the authentic aspect of Buddha's being. With the empowerment of word or logos, one realizes the "svabhavivakaya," the aspect of Buddha's being that encompasses all three, nirmanakaya, sambhogakaya, and dharmakaya. This state refers to the coming together of emptiness, luminosity, clear light, and bliss. In this particular case, the bliss that one experiences is great bliss and not contingent on any practice of union. It refers to simply being in the natural state of being. One does not use any technique or object of meditation. There are no visualizations. One simply allows oneself to be in one's own natural state, without intentional objects (Tib. *me migpa*). In relation to the fourth empowerment, one realizes the non-separability of emptiness and luminosity and emptiness and bliss. Remaining in that state is the result of word empowerment and is the same as Mahamudra. While the third empowerment enables the individual to practice karmamudra or jnanamudra, the fourth empowerment enables one to practice Mahamudra and realize Mahamudrahood. So, the last two empowerments enable the individual to practice those mudras (Tib. *chak gya*).

This basically covers the entire empowerments one needs in order to practice all aspects of the Highest Yoga Tantra of Buddhism. It does not matter what one is initiated into, if one is initiated into any practice of Highest Yoga Tantra, one has to receive these four empowerments. However, if one receives these four in relation to one tantric cycle, for example, Chakrasamvara, this does not automatically qualify one to practice another cycle of tantra. In order to do another practice, for example Hevajra tantra,[32] one must receive these empowerments again. One has to receive all of the empowerments in relation to that particular cycle of tantra and be initiated into each deity mandala. Receiving just one set of the four sets of tantric empowerments does not automatically qualify one to practice all the tantras.

The four classes of empowerments encompass all the types of empowerments a tantric practitioner must practice. Each mandala is like a self-enclosed universe. Even if one is given permission to enter into one mandala and this permission was given to enable one to explore all aspects of that particular deity yoga practice, when one wants to enter into another mandala, one again needs to have permission to enter into it because that mandala, as I mentioned, is like a self-enclosed universe.

In the tantric mandala, we have the palace in the middle and the main deity residing inside it. The palace and the main deity represent oneself and the deity inseparably together. That central palace is surrounded by various other items, which one has to visualize. It is arranged like a complete royal court. This, in itself, has symbolic meaning, which gives a sense of richness, royalty, and dignity. The mandala is enclosed; it is completely closed off from outside influences. It is similar to virtual reality video games; in order to play a game, you can only enter into that one. You cannot enter into another. You need new software for that to occur.

If one is visualizing Chakrasamvara with his consort, then he is the central figure and you are trying to become Chakrasamvara. There is no Hevajra. If you want to be Hevajra, you have to have the whole Hevajra entourage and set-up. It is not simply a matter of learning different visualizations. Each tantric mandala is a complete set of practices unto itself. There are elements that are in the Hevajra tantra that are not present in the Chakrasamvara, Guhyasamaja,[33] or Yamantaka tantras.[34] What one is trying to achieve in each tantric cycle is also different. How one is trying to deal with their own sense of masculinity and femininity, in terms of what feelings or attributes one is cultivating and projecting, are all dependent on what tantra one is practicing. It has to be unique and complete unto itself, from the taking of empowerments to the conclusion of that practice. If one has already received empowerments into one tantra, it is more likely that one will be able to go and practice another tantra. If one has never received Highest Yoga Tantra empowerments, to enter into the tantric mandala may be difficult. Once one has been able to practice a Highest Yoga Tantra, it will be easier to receive empowerments for another tantric cycle so that one can practice that.

Chapter Seven
The Creative-Imagination Stage

There are two main practices in Highest Yoga Tantra. One is called the practice of the creative-imagination stage (Skt. *sampatikrama*; Tib. *kyerim*) and the other is called the practice of completion or fulfillment stage (Skt. *nirpatikrama*; Tib. *zogrim*). In each instance, the Tibetan word "rim" and the Sanskrit word "krama" has the connotation of "grade." Even though it is translated as "stage," it infers a step-by-step process. With regard to the way in which the sadhana is conducted and in the visualizations, there is a beginning, middle, and end to each practice.

With both the stages of creative-imagination and fulfillment stages, the idea of "rim" has to correspond to the process of birthing and dying. I use the word "birthing" because it is not so much about "birth" as a state, but rather, the whole process of embryonic development—emerging out of the mother's womb, being born, maturing, growing old, and dying. The creative-imagination stage is modeled on this idea. The tantric practitioner is trying to realize that everything we experience goes through this type of process. Due to our egoistic tendency to habitually perceive things in a particular way, we are unable to appreciate how everything is constantly evolving and being propelled.

In reality, there is nothing that remains still and this contemplation is central to deity yoga practice. We consider the process of birth; we were conceived and went through the embryonic and other development stages until we were born. We were not born fully-grown but went through a process of physically growing and maturing. In relation to death, we consider the deterioration and dying process. One's life is not normally ended instantly. There is a gradual phasing out of the consciousness. This model—coming into and going out of existence—is used in the practice of "kyerim" or the creative-imagination stage.

Four different kinds of birth are mentioned in the Buddhist healing arts of medicine. The first is called "birth from the womb." Here, according to tantric and Tibetan medical texts, while the male and female are in sexual union, the consciousness of the unborn child is stirred due to sexual desire. As a result of this sexual congress, the mixing of the "red element" from the mother and the "white element" from the father occurs, at which point conception takes place.

In a similar fashion, if we visualize the deity according to the process of birth from the womb, we first visualize a sun disk and a moon disk. The sun disk represents the female element and the moon disk represents the male element. Upon the disk, one visualizes the seed syllable of the respective deity, which is single syllable, like "TAM" or "HUNG." This syllable is like the embryo or the seed of the deity. From this ensues the full development of the form of the deity.

The second variety of birth is called "birth from an egg." Some sentient creatures are born in eggshells, such as reptiles and bird species. In this case, mixing of the male and female elements, and conception and so forth, occur simultaneously. In a similar way, if we visualize the deity according to this method, we visualize the sun disk, moon disk, and seed syllable together simultaneously. Then we give rise to the deity based on that mixture.

The third category of birth is called "birth from heat and moisture." This refers to basic organisms that assume life forms without an explicit sexual act. In a similar way, we can visualize the deity in a simple manner. There is only the moon disk upon which the seed syllable is visualized. Giving rise to the deity from the moon disk and seed syllable spontaneously, is seen as comparable to birth from "moisture and heat."

The fourth mode of taking birth, according to tantric medical texts, is called "miraculous birth." This simply means that there are no observable causal conditions present for the life form to arise. They are not detected with the naked eye. When we visualize the deity corresponding to this mode, we not do not visualize the sun disk, moon disk, seed syllable, and so on, but rather, we give rise to a fully formed figure of a deity from the state of the natural clarity of bliss, the luminosity of the mind.

It is important to be aware that there are different ways to visualize deities. Tibetan thangka paintings often portray deities standing or sitting on a moon or sun disk, or both. While this type of visualization is common, it does not always involve these items. There is variation in the visualization depending on the type of practice being performed.

Normally, the visualization of the deity requires five steps known as "five factors of purity." The sun and moon disks should be resting on a lotus. So first one imagines that the sun and moon disk arise from the Tibetan alphabet, often from the vowels, as they are seen as mantras, or sacred letters. After the lotus, sun, and moon disks are visualized, the third step is the manifestation of the special implement held by the deity. Fourth, light radiates from the implement and extends outward. The light is then gathered back in and finally, the deity manifests.

According to tantric teachings, the sun and moon disks represent "mirror-like wisdom," the combination of the sun and the moon represents the "wisdom of equanimity," the seed syllable represents the "wisdom of discrimination," the implement represents the "wisdom of accomplishment," and the fully-formed body of the deity represents the "wisdom of ultimate truth."

Firstly, when visualizing oneself as the deity, we turn everything into emptiness. Due to our delusions and ignorance, everything we normally perceive is from "impure perception." In order to be able to have the experience of "pure perception," we have to deconstruct our normal perception. This is done while uttering the mantra of emptiness: "OM SVABHAVA SHUDDHA SARVA DHARMA SVABHAVA SHUDDHO HAM." One gives rise to the lotus throne out of this emptiness and then visualizes the sun and moon disks resting on top. Then one visualizes the seed syllable and subsequently, light radiating outward from the seed syllable and gathering back in again. Following this, the deity manifests. The three centers of the deity—forehead, throat, and heart centers—are marked with the three syllables "OM," "AH," and "HUM." Visualizing oneself as the deity in this way is called the *samayasattva* or "deity of commitment," because one is using oneself as the basis for the visualization.

To complete the practice of creative-imagination, one must visualize another replica of the deity, which is called the *jnanasattva* or "deity of wisdom." While you are visualizing and experiencing yourself as this particular deity, you invite the replica, the "deity of wisdom" to manifest in front of you. The "deity of wisdom" is then absorbed into you. When the deity, first visualized outside of you, is then absorbed into you, you become one with the deity. One should feel that the wisdom deity has empowered you. Once you feel empowered, you should make supplications and other prescribed prayers of appreciation.

How the jnanasattva is invited into oneself varies. Sometimes, one simply invites the deity into oneself. At other times, we imagine the deity residing in a celestial mansion or similar ethereal and enriched environment. Or it may involve more elaborate forms of visualization. The reason why one needs to invite the same deity that one has already visualized oneself to be to take residence within is because the wisdom deity should be seen as the embodiment of the enlightened mind. It is done to reinforce the conviction that one can, in fact, become enlightened. One can, in fact, manifest the same wisdom as the deity, which is the wisdom of all enlightened beings. It reinforces the fact that enlightenment is realizable. It also reinforces the sense of union, the non-separability of oneself and the wisdom of enlightenment. It helps to collapse the dualistic notion that separates our perception of ourselves from the wisdom of enlightenment, seeing it as something "other." It also has the additional purpose of developing divine pride. By developing divine pride, one becomes blessed by that deity.

This does not mean that the samayasattva—what one has visualized oneself to be, is inferior to the jnanasattva—wisdom deity, or that one becomes elevated when the wisdom deity descends into oneself. It would be mistaken to understand the distinction between the samayasattva and the jnanasattva in that way. This visualization is done to reinforce the notion of inseparability. It is not done to elevate and transform samayasattva through having received the jnanasattva.

As we want to transform our so-called "five poisons," the conflicting emotions of excessive desire, anger, jealousy, pride, and ignorance,[35] we visualize the relevant Buddha family so that the particular emotion in question will become transformed. For instance, in order to overcome anger and generate this consciousness of the deity, we visualize Akshobhya, who is the central figure of that family. In order to transform the conflicting emotion of anger, within Tantra, we invite Akshobhya to help the anger transform.

The deity one is visualized as will belong to a particular Buddha family. One can also then use a deity from another family and add it to the original deity visualization. This practice is called "affixation." One may have visualized oneself to be a particular deity of the Vajra Buddha family for example, and then one may take another deity from the Padma Buddha family and affix it to the already existing Vajra deity. Another example is that if one visualizes oneself to be Vairocana or "Boundless Light" and then affixes Akshobhya or "Unwavering" to Vairocana, one has affixed the purified body, as represented by Vairocana, with the purified mind, as represented by Akshobhya. If one has visualized oneself as Akshobhya, that can be "affixed" with Vairocana. Both of these deities are members of the five Buddha families.

It is said that we can also do "affixation" in relation to cause and effect. For instance, in order to purify the effect of jealousy, Amogasiddhi or "All-accomplishment" is used. Amogasiddhi is then affixed with Amitabha or "Infinite Light" for the purification of desire. That is the method of "effect to cause." With "cause to effect" for example, Amitabha, who represents the cause of the purification of desire, is affixed with Ratnasambhava or "Born from Jewels," who represents the effect of the purification of miserliness.

This is also explained in tantras such as the *Hevajra Tantra*. It explains how one can practice with varying combination of deities from the Buddha families within the creative-imagination stage. The deity's mudra and seed syllable identifies which Buddha family is being represented.

Deity Yoga and the Bardo State

The creative-imagination practice is designed to help us develop the ability to purify our psychophysical constituents and sensory and mental faculties. It also helps us develop the ability to manifest the power of the five wisdoms. At the time of death, if we have done the practice of creative-imagination, we will not have a frightful journey during the *bardo* or intermediate stage. It is said that if we do deity yoga practice, it will help us in our journey through the dying process and the time between death and rebirth, or in the post-mortem and pre-natal states.

As far as tantric and Tibetan medical literature is concerned, the dying process begins with the dissolution of the elements. We are made up of five elements. The solidity of the body is the earth element, the fluid in our body is the water element, the warmth in our body is the fire element, the breath in our body is the wind element, and the cavities in our body are the space element. When we are dying, the element of earth dissolves into the element of water. The external sign is that the individual begins to lose all volition and control of their body. The internal sign or the subjective experience of the dying individual is everything appearing smoky within their immediate environment. Next, the water element dissolves into the fire element. The external sign is the mouth becoming dry. The subjective experience is "mirage-like" quasi-visual apparitions. The fire element then dissolves into the wind element. At this point, the external sign is the body begins to lose heat. Subjectively, one experiences an apparition similar to fireflies. Following this, the wind element dissolves into the consciousness. The external sign of one's impending death is labored breathing—difficulty inhaling after expelling. The subjective experience is seeing an "unwavering lamp." As the consciousness itself begins to fade, the subjective experience is like "looking at a cloudless sky." This appearance dissolves into another quasi-visual apparition of "seeing everything as red." That apparition ceases and becomes absorbed into a state where one experiences a "cloudless sky without clarity," like looking into a dark sky.

At this point, the individual ceases to have any experience and becomes unconscious for a time. Then they begin to have an experience of the clear light or luminosity of the mind, which is so crisp and clear it is as if one is seeing the sky first thing in the morning, completely free of clouds. The individual then regains consciousness, based on that very simple state of cognition, which is luminosity.

From there, the consciousness becomes activated again and one has the reverse experience of the earlier dying process. At first, one has an experience that is like looking into a dark sky, then one sees everything as being red, and then one sees what appears as a cloudless sky lit up by moonlight. After death, once the reversal process is experienced, one has become a "bardo being."[36] From that, discursive thoughts begin to arise.

The first part of the bardo experience constitutes retrospective viewing of past situations and circumstances. Gradually, as time passes, these experiences begin to diminish in vivacity and one begins to have visions and images in the mind that relate to the future. The bardo being is embodied with a "bardo body," which is fully endowed with all the sense faculties. Bardo beings can perceive each other's physical forms. However, it is said in the literature that bardo beings are extremely panicky, always darting about, and searching for the next rebirth. Even though they have the common experience of being in the bardo, bardo beings each have different experiences, because each is equipped with specific ways of interpreting their own unique experiences based on their karmic inheritance. According to the teachings on bardo, the bardo being is supposed to remain in the bardo for up to seven days. If they do not succeed in finding an appropriate birth, they pass out from time to time. They have small deaths from which they get revived again. This occurs until they are able to secure the next life. If bardo beings are unsuccessful in securing rebirth easily, they may have to go through this process for approximately forty-nine days. After this time, they should have been able to find their designated rebirth.

After the bardo being has been successful in finding a rebirth, if that bardo rebirth is to be as a human being, it sees its future parents in sexual congress as the mixing of the male and female elements of conception is occurring. Within a week, the embryo starts to assume a visible form. Within five months, the embryo has developed limbs and so forth. By the seventh month, hair, nails, and so on have begun to grow. By the eighth month, the fetus has already developed eyes, nose, tongue, et cetera. By the ninth month, it is ready to take birth. The three stages in that whole process of dying, going through the journey of bardo, and rebirth are collectively known as the "basis of purification" of creative-imagination practice in Vajrayana.

The creative-imagination practice corresponds to the rebirthing process as just described, where first, one visualizes the seed syllable, then one visualizes the implement, et cetera, and gradually these give rise to the fully formed deity. These stages correspond to the various stages of the embryo and fetus. The practice of deity yoga, in relation to the samayasattva, corresponds to the development of the physical body, while the practice of the jnanasattva corresponds to the development of the psychophysical pathways and psychophysical energy centers within the body.

When we do deity yoga practice, the notion of having the deity mandala vividly present is important and so is the notion of having divine pride to go along with that. Deity yoga practice should be used to develop mindfulness. One should not only be able to visualize the deity vividly, but also properly recite the mantras and do whatever the sadhana requires. One should practice with vigor and conviction. If a distraction occurs during the visualization practice, one should not yield to the distraction, but return quickly to the visualization of the deity. If we have problems visualizing deities, we can think of the qualities the deity possesses, such as compassion, wrath, et cetera—whatever qualities are associated with that particular deity. Also, one can focus on a physical aspect of the deity one at a time, such as the face, hand mudras, et cetera, and try to bring that to a certain level of vivacity. The use of Tibetan thangkas, painted scrolls, and detailed photographs, can be helpful. One can return to that image repeatedly properly examining the details. After studying the picture, one can repeatedly close one's eyes and turn away, to make the image reappear in one's mind, just like a lustful person who is repeatedly thinking of the person they are attracted to causing the person's image to come into their mind.

Much of this process is a case of practice and familiarization. If one becomes familiar with the practice, the visualization itself will become easier and the mind will naturally tend toward a clearer perception. Just like an actor in a play, playing the role repeatedly can make projecting the persona needed for that particular role more natural and potent. Similarly, with persistence, minor difficulties such as the visualization being unclear will be overcome as familiarity with the practice grows and the visualization naturally becomes clearer. This is also discussed in the sutric teachings. For example, it states that whatever we obsessively think about, irrespective of whether it is good or bad, because of familiarity can be seen clearly in the mind without difficulty.

Having established the importance of being persistent with deity yoga practices, it should be remembered the practices are not an end in themselves. Deity yoga is purely and importantly a helpful device to develop certain positive and transformative states of mind. It is not the ultimate goal of one's spiritual practice. In relation to the deities and the mandalas they occupy, we need to keep in mind that they are devoid of inherent existence. They do not have any real nature, therefore are not absolute representations of reality. They are more comparable to magic illusions or reflections of the moon on the surface of water. It should be remembered that the deities can potently effect change within the individual practitioner. In that way, we should recognize the deities as neither truly existent, nor completely non-existent.

While doing deity yoga practice, we should keep in mind that it is a purification practice. Engaging in this practice is what enables us to purify and transcend all manner of shortcomings and defective qualities. We should think that one's body, speech, mind, and all of the psychophysical constituents upon which our identity is based, have been transformed. While visualizing the deities in the creative-imagination stage, we should think that these deities are manifestations of our innate nature. Our innate nature is the non-divisibility of bliss and emptiness, called the co-emergent clear light of bliss, also known as reflexive awareness. This clear light of bliss is seen as pure within its own nature. It is not pure because certain defilements have been removed from it. The clear light of bliss is an innate state of wakefulness that has the capacity to purify all defilements, bringing one to the realization of the self-cognizing awareness of great bliss.

The Mantric Aspect of Deity Yoga

The different practices include specific instructions about the correct type of mala to use when reciting mantras. In Tantrism, mantras are recited for different reasons—for pacification, empowerment, expansion, and subjugation. So one needs to develop skill to recite mantras effectively. Knowing the mantra is not sufficient.

If one is engaged in the practice of a peaceful deity, one recites the mantra in keeping with that deity. The mala that one uses in this instance should be made of crystal, pearl, or be white in color. This accomplishes the function of pacification. Malas made of precious matter such as gold, silver, copper, or even lotus roots are used to fulfill the function of expansion, with the relevant deity yoga practice. For the function of empowering, one uses malas made from materials that are aromatic, such as sandalwood, or treated with aromatic substances such as saffron. In order to fulfill the function of subjugation through wrathful means, one uses a mala made from bones or the rudraksha seed that the Indian sadhus use. The best way to do all of these practices with only one mala is to use one made from bodhi seeds.

It is also said in tantric texts that the number of beads on the different types of malas is important. One uses fifty beads for the empowering mala, one hundred beads for pacification, one hundred and eight beads for expansion, and sixty beads for subjugation. There are also specifications regarding the length of string, how to roll the beads when one counts them, how to bless each mala, and how to count the number of times one has rolled the beads. For instance, if one is doing a peaceful practice and reciting the mantra of a peaceful deity, the mala should be rotated while resting on the forefinger. For expansion, it has to be rotated while resting on the middle finger. For empowering, the mala should be rotated while resting on the forefinger. Lastly, for the purpose of subjugation, the mala should be rolled using the thumb in the shape of a hook while making a circular motion of summoning.

Also specified is the way in which mantras are recited. One way of reciting the mantra is the "inhalation and exhalation" method. Here, the mantra is recited while imagining that there is a seed syllable resting on a sun and moon disk in one's heart center, and that emanations or replicas of the deity issue forth and spread in all directions. While one is breathing out, one should imagine that these multiples of emanations of that deity have spread out in all directions fulfilling the needs and wishes of everyone. When one inhales, they are all gathered back and absorbed back into the seed syllable at one's heart center. While doing this visualization practice and recitation, one should think that the whole host of these deities is pleased and joyous.

One can also use the "mala of mantra" method. Here, one recites the mantra while imagining that everything that exists in the world of space and time exists in a state of equanimity. As you recite the mantras, you visualize the deity in the space before you, with the seed syllable of the deity, and the mantra of the deity, circling it in a clockwise direction, in the heart center of that deity. For example, if you were visualizing Vajrasattva, whose mantra is "OM VAJRA SATTVA HUM," you would have the seed syllable "HUM" in the middle and "OM VAJRA SATTVA HUM" circling it in a clockwise direction at Vajrasattva's heart center. Then you imagine that the seed syllable and the mantra circle out of Vajrasattva's heart and enter your body through your mouth. The mantra then exits through the sexual organ and returns to Vajrasattva. It enters into the deity through their sexual organ and emerges again from the mouth of the deity. This happens in a circular motion and creates a circle of mantra. One should recite the mantra while concentrating on that.

One can also recite the mantra in another way. Instead of *receiving* the mala mantra through the mouth, the mantra *exits* through one's mouth and enters the mouth of the deity. The mantra then reappears through the genitals of the deity and enters through one's own genitals. Again, the mantra circles in that motion. This is called the "mantra recitation of a fire ring." An analogy for this would be lighting a stick of incense and quickly whirling it around in the air so that you get the visual impression of a fire ring. The color that the mantra will have depends upon the deity and the Buddha family the deity belongs to.

We recite the mantra in different ways but the real mantra is the seed syllable or *bija* mantra. The seed syllable represents the very essence of the deity. Recitation is done to activate the essence of the deity. It also anchors the mind to one's natural state, the clear light of bliss. It also helps prevent distractions. The mantras we recite are designed to activate the essence of the three aspects of Buddha's being—body, speech, and mind.

We should pay attention to how we are reciting the mantra. Is it too fast, slow, or loud? Is there enough energy behind the recitation? Is one enunciating the mantra properly so that the vowels are pronounced and accented? Is one interrupting the recitation to engage in conversation with someone nearby? Is one reciting the mantra while in a distracted state? When we recite the mantra, we should not recite it either too slowly or quickly. Whether we are exhaling or inhaling should not affect the tone of the recitation. Nor does it lead to mental clarity to force the recitation and recite it very loudly. When done well, mantra recitation guards against our tendency to get caught up in an agitated state of mind and disturbing emotions. When we recite the mantra in a meditative state, all of the conditions can come together to develop the qualities of the deity and the qualities and attributes of enlightenment.

The recitation of mantras serves three fundamental functions. First, uttering the mantra is like calling someone's name, in this case it is the name of the deity. Second, mantras help to arrest unruly conflicting emotions. Third, mantras are like invitations for the states of awakening to arise. Reciting mantras in a proper fashion elicits both temporal and ultimate enlightened energies.

Deity Practice In Retreat

In a retreat environment when seriously engaging in tantric practice, one's day is traditionally divided into four segments. They consist of a session at dawn, morning to midday, afternoon session, and a final session in the evening.

There are three stages of the deity practice to be performed in each session, the initial preparatory stage, the actual practice, and concluding in the proper manner through the dissolution of the visualization.

As previously mentioned, the dissolution stage in deity yoga corresponds to the actual dying process. At the time of death, we experience the dissolution of the elements until only the subtle clear light is present. This is followed by the dissolution of the consciousness and the bardo physical embodiment. Similarly, with the deity practice, we should first dissolve and absorb the entire external world into oneself. The external world contains sentient creatures that all dissolved into oneself. Then we should gradually dissolve ourselves and the visualization. This corresponds to the dissolution of the elements in the dying process. Everything dissolves into the state of luminous clarity. We remain in that state of luminous clarity for a short time. This state is comparable to being in the bardo, one should rouse from that state in the form of the deity one was just visualizing. As the deity, one distributes offerings of *balingta* or offering cakes to satisfy living beings who are hungry, distressed, and experiencing other forms of extreme suffering. One concludes the session by offering balingta, which is done to clear any obstacles in the course of one's practice.

The dedication prayer is then recited to complete the session, wishing that one's deity practice and recitation of mantras completed in the session help to generate positive states of mind and positive dispositional qualities. One should wish that all of this contributes to actualizing the state of Buddhahood without any spiritual activity going to waste. By dedicating the merit of one's practice in this way, one would seek to achieve the fruit of both temporary and ultimate happiness. Through such dedication, we are planting the seed for the achievement of Buddhahood. As it is said in Buddhist teachings, the dedication of merit is like putting a drop of water in the ocean. Just as long as the ocean remains, the drop of water that has gone into it will remain. Similarly, if one dedicates whatever merit one has accumulated up to this point to the sole purpose of achieving Buddhahood, none of the merit that has been accumulated will ever go to waste until that state is attained.

The final reminder in deity practice is to remember one's deity in the post-meditation state. In daily life, one should think of oneself as that deity, embodying their qualities whenever possible. If we are able to do that, our physical movement is like a mudra and our speech becomes a mantric sound. Even when eating, one should eat with a sense of mindfulness. One dedicates the food for the welfare of others and thinks, "Any indebtedness I feel towards others is dissolved within this dedication." Then think, "May I instantly realize the deity fully." So one is always reminding oneself of and seeing oneself as the deity, embodying their qualities, seeing everything as being within the deity's mandala, and hearing everything as the sound of the mantra of the deity. We should consecrate food as a ritual feast and see the substances as being consumed by the mystic heat in one's body, in the form of the deity.

When going to sleep, retain a sense of mindfulness and try to dissolve all of one's external perceptions into luminous clarity. Then generate the co-emergent bliss and luminosity in the state of emptiness and try to drift into that state as one goes to sleep. In order to help achieve this co-emergence, one can visualize the syllable "HUM" at the heart center and concentrate on that to help maintain a sense of luminous clarity, and then one dissolves everything into the "HUM" syllable. Then, without thinking about anything, one should drift into sleep.

One should try to wake up with a sense of sacred outlook, think that four celestial dakinis or goddesses are singing, and then wake up in the form of the deity. The "four goddesses," in fact refer to the four *Brahmaviharas*, the four infinities of love, compassion, joy, and equanimity. Through their encouragement, one engages with the world.

The main point is to maintain a sense of sacred outlook. We try to avoid automatically drifting into a state of normal, impure perceptions. During the course of the day, try to always maintain the sense that everything that one perceives is illusion-like and try to maintain a meditative state as much as one is able.

Chapter Eight
Mystic Heat Yoga and the Completion Stage

The second arm of Buddhist tantric practice is known as the fulfillment stage, or the stage of completion. This practice has two aspects, which also signifies the notion of *rimpa* or *rim*, "stage" or "grade." The first aspect is the practice of mystic heat yoga, (Tib. tummo; Skt. chandali). The second aspect is called illusory body yoga. You may be familiar with the Six Yogas of Naropa[37] and the Six Yogas of Niguma, who is traditionally said to be Naropa's sister. Some have said that Niguma was not his sister, but rather his secret consort. In ancient India, it was not uncommon for a consort to be referred to as "sister." Whichever the case may be, the Six Yogas that have come down to us from Naropa and Niguma are regarded as particularly important in the Kagyu tradition of Tibetan Buddhism. These Six Yogas are also included in the two practices of mystic heat yoga and illusory body yoga. The Six Yogas of Naropa will be discussed in detail in section two.

From the perspective of "rimpa," mystic heat yoga is not as profound as that of illusory body yoga. Mystic heat yoga deals with our relative nature, in relation to what is called our "subtle body." This means that it is not a gross body of flesh, bones, blood, veins, and so on, but rather a subtle body in terms of our psychophysical energy pathways (Skt. *nadi*), psychophysical energy (Skt. *prana*) and life essence (Skt. *bindu*). The subtle body however, is still dealing with our relative condition. On the other hand, with illusory body yoga, we are seeking to realize our true nature, ultimate truth. In that way, illusory body yoga is seen as more profound.

Tibetan mystic heat yoga is called "tummo" in Tibetan. *Tum* means "ferocious" and *mo* means "feminine," so "tummo" means "ferocious female energy." The ferocity here also has the implication of heat, like a furiously raging fire. What we have to realize is that through the generation of this heat in the practice of mystic heat yoga, one can experience the clear light of bliss. This is accomplished by working with the psychophysical pathways (Tib. *tsa*; Skt. *nadi*), the psychophysical energy, often translated as "winds" (Tib. *lung*; Skt. *prana*), and the life essence (Tib. *thigle*; Skt. *bindu*). Through the integration of these three, one can reach the level of experiencing the clear light of bliss, which according to Tantrism, is the experience of our own true nature.

Mystic heat yoga practice is designed to channel the psychophysical energy or prana into the central psychophysical energy pathway or nadi. When the prana enters into the central psychophysical energy pathways or nadis, one has four different kinds of experiences in succession. These are known as the "four empties." However, it is important to note that "empties" does not mean the realization of "emptiness" (Skt. *shunyata*) as it is understood in Mahayana Buddhism.[38] The four empties refer to the gradual decrease in certain mental functionings. In order to achieve that, we need to learn to stabilize the life essence or bindu.

In order to learn how to control and manipulate the flow of the psychophysical energy, we also have to gain some appreciation for the psychophysical pathways. Apart from the central psychophysical energy pathways, which are positioned in the center of one's body, parallel to the spinal column, are thousands of networks of psychophysical energy pathways serving as conduits for the flow of psychophysical energy. It is said that for the flow of the functioning of one's life force, there are about 24,000 different energy pathways. For the circulation of blood, there are another 24,000, and for the circulation of the psychophysical energy, another 24,000. This amounts to approximately 72,000 networks of psychophysical energy pathways. In the tantric literature, it is said that these are the main conduits for the functioning of one's body, but there are also many smaller pathways that literally run into the millions.

If we take only those that are the most significant, we have about 120 networks of energy pathways that crisscross at the four psychophysical energy centers or chakras, various points of the subtle body. From these 120, there are three main psychophysical energy pathways. In terms of one's practice, these three nadis and four chakras are very significant. There are also different types of prana. There is the psychophysical energy that moves downward and psychophysical energy that moves upward. There is the prana that pervades the whole of one's subtle body, the prana of evenness, which controls bodily temperature, and so forth, and there is the prana of life essence (Skt. *bindu*).

The bindu or life essence refers to the "breath." When we breathe through our nostrils for instance, the essence of psychophysical energy is the bindu or life essence, and our breathing. These are the most significant precisely because our life literally depends them. According to tantric literature, our consciousness attaches itself to the essence of the psychophysical energy of life essence. How the psychophysical energy is circulating in one's body and how one's breathing pattern is conducted would be reflected in how our mind is functioning and in our states of consciousness.[39] The downward moving prana helps us to purify our psychophysical system by ejecting bodily waste, and so forth. The upward moving prana can also give us the function of being able to cough, eject mucus, et cetera from the body. The all-pervading psychophysical energy and the psychophysical energy of evenness control our digestive system, monitor the temperature of the body, and the like.

In the practice of mystic heat yoga, one learns to work with three of the five psychophysical energies namely the upward moving prana, the downward moving prana, and the psychophysical energy of life essence. Mystic heat practice enables one to learn to use the potency of these three psychophysical energies by perfecting the art of breathing. There are four factors involved in the practice: how one inhales, holds the breath, moves the energy, and forcefully exhales the breath. One's proficiency with these breathing exercises will determine how skilled one becomes in mastering the yoga of psychophysical energy (Skt. *pranayama*).

Here we are dealing with two kinds of life essence or bindu—female and male. Both of these travel through 24,000 energy pathways. According to some tantric texts, the male element is circulated mostly in thirty-two of these. The source of this male life essence lies in the crown region of the subtle body. The female life essence on the other hand, resides in the abdominal region. Mystic heat yoga activates the female life essence with the proper controlling and processing of the psychophysical energy or prana. The heat from this rises upward, which then melts the male life essence in the crown center.

This has to be understood in a symbolic fashion. Nothing literally melts in the head. It is more a sense of the subtle workings of the body, both in the rising of the female element and the descending of the male element. One will succeed in doing this only if one has been able to direct the psychophysical energy into the central energy pathway. As the psychophysical energy enters into the central psychophysical energy channel, one has the experience of both heat and bliss. It is said in various tantric texts that there are various points in the subtle body, where the psychophysical energy centers or chakras are located. This is where it is possible for the psychophysical energy to enter the central psychophysical energy pathway. In the practice of mystic heat yoga however, the tantric sadhaka attempts to make the psychophysical energy enter mainly through the psychophysical center in the abdominal region, where the female energy is located.

When this is achieved, one will have experiences that correspond to the dissolution stages mentioned earlier. As a sign that the psychophysical energy has entered the central energy pathway, one will experience quasi-visual perceptions that reflect the dissolution of the elements. Due to the dissolution of the earth element, one will experience a quasi-visual perception of a mirage. With the dissolution of the water element, one will experience a perception of smokiness. The dissolution of the fire element will produce the perception of firefly apparition. The dissolution of the wind element will produce an apparition that is lamp-like. And finally, when the consciousness is dissolved, one will have perception like space without clouds.

One can reverse this process and have the same experiences successively in reverse order. There are several different methods that are employed to effect this process. One has to first visualize the three psychophysical energy pathways and four psychophysical energy centers. Then one has to think that the mystic heat resides in the abdominal region and that one has to fan it with the psychophysical energy. However, one may not be able to easily succeed at this simply by thinking about it or imagining it to be there, so visualization methods are used to aid one with the activation of the heat. One does this by visualizing seed syllables. One can visualize the seed syllables *AH* at the abdominal chakra, *HUNG* at the heart chakra, *OM* at the throat chakra, and an upside down *HUNG* at the head chakra. One focuses one's mind on those visualizations, using the mantric syllables as a means of anchoring one's attention. Then one should think that as the heat begins to rise, the inverted *HUNG* begins to melt. This provides a vivid image for the practice. Vivid imagery is important. If one is not visualizing but thinking that the male element in the crown is melting and the heat is rising, one may not experience much. It is important for the practice to include a quasi-visual aid to help to have a full experience. With the help of this visualization, the inverted *HUNG* will begin to melt and one will experience a degree of samadhi or meditative concentration known as "the non-divisibility of bliss and emptiness."

There are many different ways of doing this practice, from simple practices such as the one just described, to the more detailed visualizations that include numerous seed syllables, or miniature deities located at different points in one's body. In this last visualization of miniature deities, one imagines female and male deities populating all of the extremities of one's subtle body. This visualization is not necessary, but it may be of use.

In the tantric system, the point to both the creative-imagination stage and the completion stage is to attain an extremely subtle state of non-discursive thought. It is said that if the individual's mind is always extremely active and constantly thinking, then even engaging in visualization practices will still not be sufficient and one's normal, everyday thoughts start to intrude. If the visualization becomes highly complex however, there are so many things to think about that every second is taken up by something. Then, because your mind is constantly occupied, you are in a meditative state and have no time to wander and allow your mind to become distracted.

In this practice, one should also visualize oneself as a deity but unlike the creative-imagination stage, one should not worry too much about building the visualization up from something simple such as a seed syllable. Instead, one should see oneself as a specific deity and then think that this deity is illusion-like. This basically means that that deity is vividly present, yet insubstantial from the beginning of the visualization. One then has to visualize the three psychophysical energy pathways or nadis and the four psychophysical energy centers or chakras. In the crown center, one visualizes the seed syllable *HUNG* and in the abdominal region, the mystic heat. Then, it is with the use of the upward moving and downward moving psychophysical energy along with the visualization that causes the production of bliss, luminosity, and clarity.

From this, one will experience the four different types of ecstasies, which are joy, bliss, ecstasy, and then co-emergent bliss and ecstasy. These four different types of ecstasies are obtained when the motility breaks through at each of the chakras, from the crown to the throat, from the throat to the heart, and from the heart to below the navel region to the genital region. The bliss is controlled at that point and then reversed backward. Then the psychophysical energy is pushed back through the central channels and travels back through the specific psychophysical energy centers of the body. As such, bliss is experienced with both the ascending and descending of the prana.

The whole purpose of doing mystic heat yoga is to experience co-emergent bliss (Skt. *sahaja sukha*) because co-emergent bliss will lead to the realization of clear light of bliss. All other types of bliss or ecstasy are not complete. They are generated to approximate the full bliss experience of co-emergent bliss. This co-emergent bliss when realized, is the experience of non-duality, where there is no separation between bliss and clear light. Both clear light and bliss are revealed to be the same. This break through, this luminous experience, is referred to as the realization of "wisdom mystic heat." This is the essence of tummo. Other techniques help lead us to this realization. There is no notion of duality within this experience. There is no separation between oneself as the subject having the experience and that which is experienced. Even the subtlest forms of dualistic notions have vanished. All dualities would be revealed as co-emergent. In other words, without subject and object, the true essence of everything is revealed as co-emergent bliss.

To engage in an extremely profitable way with mystic heat yoga, one needs the relevant instructions from one's vajracharya. One's success in this practice is determined only by the confidence of one's teacher and one's own aptitude. If one does not relate properly to the practice, one will not profit from practicing it. Nor would one profit from it if the teacher providing the instructions is not properly qualified.

As can be seen from what we have said so far about mystic heat yoga, a lot of the practices of the Six Yogas are present within it. The Six Yogas as a group are something that arose at a later time in history. Many people have the notion that all of the tantric systems somehow arose simultaneously. However, tantric practices went through various stages of development, refinement, systematization, codification, and so forth. The six practices are a skillful method for helping us to practice Tantra more effectively. They are simply a more expanded version of the practices already described here.

Chapter Nine
The Completion Stage Practices

We touched on the notion of great "rim pa," or "rim" for short, in Tibetan, which means that the different stages of tantric practice are ordered in relation to both the profundity and the subtlety of the practices. The grosser and more elaborate practices are graded lower than the simpler, less elaborate ones. As one begins to become more familiar with tantric practices and is introduced to very elaborate forms of visualization, recitations of mantras, mudras, and so forth, one should not assume that these forms of practice are extremely advanced. The more elaborate forms of practice are designed to deal with an already exceedingly busy mind and its proliferations of thoughts and concepts. As one begins to progress with tantric practice, one becomes more and more familiar with subtle levels of consciousness where the proliferation of discursive thoughts begins to decrease. Then one has more experience of the clear light of bliss, which is one's true state of being. Whatever is taking place on the grosser level of mental activities is only at the surface of the mind.

Each tantric practice has gross to subtle levels. That is why the creative-imagination stage has levels or steps within it that are graded from gross to subtle to very subtle. The completion stage is also graded in terms of mystic heat yoga. This has gross and subtle level of visualizations and practices igniting different kinds of bliss experiences leading to co-emergent bliss. After accessing these subtler levels of consciousness, one moves onto the next practice of illusory body yoga. Again, this is graded in terms of gross and subtle levels of practice. When we look at tantric practice as a whole, there is always the gradual movement from gross levels of consciousness to subtle levels of consciousness. The final level is attained with the final completion stage. We need to keep this in mind with tantric practice.

We practice the stage of creative-imagination in order to deconstruct our normal perception of the world and ourselves, so that our normal perception, which is known as "impure perception," is replaced by the "pure perception." From a Buddhist perspective, our normal state of consciousness is fixated on what we experience through our sensory apparatuses, impressions, moods, emotions, cogitations, cognitive states of mind, conceptual categories, and schemas. All of these go toward reinforcing our fixation of our mental states. We experience everything to be very real and solid thus producing ever-increasing states of mental agitation, worry, concern, fear, and anxiety. The more we think that what we are experiencing about the world and ourselves is entirely true and real, the more we become alarmed and our suffering increases.

The practice of deity yoga can help us to realize that our perception is just a perception. This does not mean that our perceptions are completely unreal or have not happened. They have happened and do happen, but due to our fixation, we do not experience things in a genuine way. The way we engage with the world is normally narrow and limiting. We can tend to produce many unnecessary concerns. The most trivial things can assume a high degree of importance. Even a small thought can trigger a monumental response as if it were earth shattering.

We practice deity yoga to realize the relative nature of our ordinary perception, perceptions we have become accustomed to and assume represent how things really are. We come to completely rely on them as being completely true. That becomes relativized and questioned or undermined. Deity yoga practice helps to see things in a different way, from another perspective or angle. Our perceptions operate more unconsciously and within our subjective states of mind and it has an effect on how we engage with others and the world. When transformation begins to take place, we are replacing impure perception with the development of pure perception. When we become more adept at our practices, we begin to develop deeper understanding and greater insight. Even though we dissolve the visualization of deities at the end of each practice, fixation can develop regarding the notion of pure perception. With regard to one's perception of the divine embodiment of the deity, the cultivation and realization of the deity, divine pride, and so on, all these attitudes and realizations also have to be transcended.

That level of perception therefore, has to be relativized and superseded, through the practice of the completion stage. The whole notion of divine pride can be transcended through the practice of mystic heat yoga, where one works with one's subtle body in terms of psychophysical energy, psychophysical energy centers, life essence, and psychophysical energy pathways. There is the notion of dismantling one's fixation of deity yoga in this practice, because deity yoga is seen as a preparatory step for the practice of the completion stage practice. After deity yoga, one's mind should be less subjected to overwhelming discursive thoughts, so it is easier to access and to work with one's subtle energies.

With mystic heat yoga, one may have achieved certain deep, powerful, and moving experiences. There is also the possibility that one may get fixated on that. Fixation is established through thinking and conceptualizing as the means to work out what we are experiencing; "Now this is happening, now that is happening. Now I have realized this, now I have realized that." So that strong tendency also needs to be transcended and relativized. None of these practices are absolute, in any sense of the word.

Right from the beginning, the possibility has always existed that one may realize the clear light of bliss with the practice of deity yoga. In that case, there would be no need to go through these various stages of practice. However, this is less likely, so we go through the different stages to gradually access the more and more subtle levels of consciousness and in that way can realize the clear light of bliss. To achieve this goal via the tantric methods, which acknowledges that our minds are full of mental activities, states, and processes, we need all kinds of complicated systems of practice. Gradually, we can simplify the practices so that our mind becomes more manageable, and the practices become increasingly refined. The more elaborate types of tantric practices are called the outer practices, the subtler are called the inner practices, and the even subtler practices are called the secret practices. For example, outer practice is like deity yoga, inner practice is like mystic heat yoga, and secret practice is like the practice of the indivisibility of bliss and clear light, the clear light of bliss. One has to move from the gross to the subtle levels in that way. The secret practices are the most basic of all practices, even though they are the most advanced.

Illusory Body Yoga

Illusory body yoga is practiced in order to have the experience of subtle states of consciousness. In illusory body yoga, we have to learn to see everything that we perceive as illusory. This means that one has to see everything as illusion-like, both in terms of the "container" or the physical world, and the "content," or the sentient creatures contained therein. Everything should be seen as like reflections in a mirror, a dream, or magical illusion. One then visualizes one's own body as being like an image, similar to a painting, drawing, or an echo, while one's thoughts and perceptions should be as a mirage, unlike the sutric teachings. In the sutric teachings, we try to understand the non-substantiality of things through reasoning. In illusory yoga, we use the visualization techniques of creative-imagination to arrive at that same understanding.

We engage in twelve meditations, or twelve examples of illusion, to realize illusory body yoga:

1. Even though our body has no inherent substance, no enduring essence, it appears with all of its limbs and faculties, so we should think of it as a "body of illusion."

2. Because nothing has really ever come into existence with any enduring substance, we should think of everything that we perceive as "the reflection of the moon in water."

3. We should think of everything that we see as something that someone would perceive if they were "suffering from cataracts."

4. Because instability is an abiding feature of what we perceive, with everything always in a state of movement, we should meditate upon everything that we see as "like a mirage."

5. Because everything that we perceive is dependent upon the mind, we should meditate on everything as if it were "like a dream."

6. Because everything we perceive is a product of causes and conditions, we should meditate on everything as "like an echo."

7. Because there is no real determining characteristic to anything that we perceive, we should meditate on everything as "the pure hallucinatory perception of a siddha."

8. Even though nothing has substantial existence, it still appears, so we should meditate on everything "as clouds."

9. Because everything that we perceive, both internally and externally, appears clearly to the mind and is not obstructed in its nature, we should meditate on everything "as rainbows."

10. Because things move so fast and change occurs so quickly, we should meditate on everything "as lightning."

11. Because everything that we observe occurs in seconds rather than hours or minutes, we should meditate on everything "as bubbles."

12. Even though everything appears, nothing that appears to us has any reality, so we should meditate on everything "as reflections of images in a mirror."

One engages in this practice of illusory body yoga in the same way that one practices mystic heat yoga practice, so that one's psychophysical energy would start to enter into the central energy pathway and from that, the experience of the four "empties" would arise. As discussed earlier, the "empties" refer to the fact that as the psychophysical energy enters into the central energy pathway, there is a slowing down of mental agitation, which brings about the absorptive states. With the onset of the absorptive states, there is literally a cessation of certain forms of mental activity. It is the cessation of these mental activities that is called "empty." It is important to have an understanding of the empties. The series of "empties" are like states or grades. The first "state of empty" is the least profound, while the second, third, and fourth are successively more profound in nature. Just like the four blisses that I mentioned previously, the "empties" are not of the same nature. Every time there is a certain "shutdown" of certain aspects of our mental functioning, there is an experience of "empties," whose activity or lack of activity is signaled by a quasi-visual apparition. There is that correspondence between these apparitions and the eventual arrival at the level of the clear light of bliss.

The individual doing illusory body yoga has to manifest themselves in the form of a particular deity. As we are not describing a particular practice of a deity here, one should think of whichever practice it is that one is doing and imagine arising as that deity. To arise in the form of a deity from the clear light of bliss is the subtlest form of deity yoga practice. In fact, it is called the illusory body of "esotericness." While one is in this state, the movement of the psychophysical energy, energy pathways, and centers, et cetera becomes reactivated and in turn, our various levels of consciousness also become reactivated. Functioning in that way during practice is what is called the "illusory body."

One can realize the subtler or grosser level of the illusory body yoga practice, depending upon how efficient one has become. The subtle type of illusory body yoga is where the psychophysical energy enters into the central energy pathway and reaches the heart chakra until it effects the "great empty," which is one of the four "empties." This combination of psychophysical energy and the mind produces the illusory body yoga experience and one arises as the manifestation of the deity. One does not physically arise, of course, one is simply awakened or stirred, and the deity emerges from that state. This is called "original illusory body." The lesser type of illusory body yoga is when the psychophysical energy—*viau* is the term that is more commonly used in tantric texts, because prana is one of the functions of viau—enters into central energy pathway and dissipates there, producing just a "state of empty." From the combination of the psychophysical energy and consciousness, one can arise from that state in the form of a deity. This is called "provisional illusory body." The twelve meditations on illusion listed earlier can then be applied to the illusory body that one has now brought into being in the form of a deity.

The Six Yogas of Naropa

The Six Yogas of Naropa are included in these practices. Illusory body yoga can be applied to dream yoga, the yoga of the intermediary stage, and the yoga of transference of consciousness. Even though all of the other Six Yogas of Naropa can be applied to illusory body yoga, it is this illusory body yoga that is the key because it leads to the subtlest of all of our experiences regarding the natural state of the mind. Both Tilopa[40] and Naropa, who were key figures in making these practices more widespread, believed that the other four, mystic heat yoga, dream yoga, the yoga of the intermediary stage, and the yoga of transference of consciousness, were limbs of the illusory body yoga practice. The approach in these other practices is very much the same. One has to direct the psychophysical energy into the central energy pathway, which then effects the four "empties" and gives rise to the corresponding apparitions, et cetera. Once one has the experience of the clear light of bliss, one remains in that state. One also makes use of one's dream experiences as part of one's spiritual training.

The Six Yogas of Naropa

Chapter One

Overview of the Six Yogas of Naropa

The teachings on the Six Yogas of Naropa are vast and profound and sometimes held in secrecy. It is very important subject matter and belongs to the highest form of Tantrism, *Mahanuttarayoga tantra*, introduced to Tibet after the ninth century, from the tenth and eleventh century onwards. Some of the tantric masters in India were forced to take refuge in Nepal and Tibet, so many of the so-called newer tantras, all the cycles of Mahanuttarayoga tantra, were introduced by either masters that went to India to receive the teachings or Indian masters that came to Tibet and gave the teachings there. Mahanuttarayoga tantra is the form of Tantrism that developed in India late in Buddhist history. Scholars say these forms of practice took shape when Buddhism was dying out during the tenth and fourteenth centuries. By the fourteenth century, Buddhism had disappeared from its original soil, in India, but these forms of Tantrism were still very active during this time.

This, in itself, is quite interesting. Sometimes people say that it is because Buddhist Tantrism became so complex and esoteric that Buddhism died out in India. What is important is that Buddhism developed and went through many different stages and the Buddhist form of Tantrism went through various stages of development as well. In any case, the Mahanuttarayoga form of Tantrism is the most esoteric. The Six Yogas of Naropa belong to that category. The esoteric practices are esoteric for a reason. The practices are very challenging, even disturbing and confronting. The reason why something is esoteric is due to its ability to disturb and that is why it is important for the element of secrecy to be there.

As far as Tibetan teachers go, the Six Yogas of Naropa can be traced back to Marpa and before Marpa, to Naropa. The Gelug school also has the Six Yogas practice. The Six Yogas practice can also be traced back to Marpa, Milarepa, Gampopa, and Phagmo Drupa.[41] They can also be traced through the Drigung Kagyu lineage, which is a sub-sect of the Kagyu lineage. The Kagyus are supposed to be specialists in the Six Yogas. That is how it was transmitted from master to practitioner through the centuries and how this lineage was preserved, not just within the different Kagyu schools or traditions, but also the four major and the eight minor schools of the Kagyu lineage, and through the Gelug tradition.[42]

The Six Yogas are actually called the "Six Doctrines" or "Six Dharmas," (Tib. *na ro chos drug*); chos means "dharma." The word "yoga" is not normally used. In Tibetan, the word "yoga" is *rnal 'byor*. It is not called the "Six Yogas," but the "Six Doctrines." The term, "Six Yogas" was used when these texts were being translated into English. The "Six Yogas" should actually be known as the "Six Doctrines" or "Six Techniques." This would be a more accurate translation, but in this book I am adhering to current convention to avoid any unnecessary misunderstanding.

This presentation on the Six Yogas will be an introduction. I will give you a lot of information about the practices however I will not give you the manual, so to speak. To actually practice, you have to express your desire and go through the proper procedures. You have to receive empowerments and so on. Knowing what the practices are about and how they are performed is important. In Tibetan Buddhism, sometimes people may do advanced tantric practices but not know what they are doing. When the practices are not performed or understood properly, it can disturb the person or they may just want to give up, as their expectations and the wonderful things they were looking forward to may not happen. They may become bored, waiting for some kind of cosmic inner explosion. If we have this attitude, it is not going to work because it is not about taking us out of our own existential condition. It is more about going deeper into ourselves, and at the same time, managing to transcend ourselves. This is the extraordinary thing about these practices. All the techniques that are mentioned in the Six Yogas are involved with going deeper into oneself and yet at the same time, being able to transcend.

Our egoistic notion of "who we think we are" is so limited. When we go beyond that and stop thinking, "I am Paul. I am a mechanic. I'm simply an eater of food," when we go deeper into ourselves in that way, we can see we are not who or what we think we are. In that way, we go beyond what we thought was ourself. We often think that in order to go beyond ourselves, we have to get outside of ourselves, as if transcendence means leaping out of ourselves. Even the word "ecstasy" means, "getting out of oneself." It is a form of ecstasy. You are going out of your sense of yourself by going deeper into yourself. All Six Yogas emphasize this point, as we will see. This is an extremely important aspect to grasp.

We attach so much importance to what we think of ourselves, and this becomes so fixed. All Six Yogas are designed to give us the opportunity to see ourselves in a different light. We can see that what is objectively perceived and what is subjectively experienced go hand-in-hand and are not separate. What we perceive externally and what we perceive and experience internally are not separate.

This is also what is being spoken of here. When we go into an ecstatic mode in our practice, such as bliss, we are experiencing things in a non-divisible way, seeing in a different light—what is subjectively experienced and what is objectively observed.

Normally, we perceive things from the point of view of our egoistic perspective: "There's the world out there and there is me. I'm going through this and that experience, but that world is out there." The Six Yogas deconstruct that whole notion of, "the external world is out there to be observed at a distance and the subjective world is totally different, my own experience." The Six Yogas teach that there is no disconnection.

Mystic Heat Yoga

The first yoga that I will be talking about is *chandali* or *tummo* practice, mystic heat yoga. Following this is dream yoga, the yoga of clear light or luminosity, and illusory body yoga. These four yogas are seen as the main practices of the Six Yogas of Naropa. The last two, *bardo* or intermediate stage and *phowa* or transference of consciousness, are auxiliary to the main practice of the first four: mystic heat yoga, dream yoga, yoga of clear light, and illusory body yoga.

Mystic heat yoga or tummo is the most important of the yogas in the Kagyu lineage. It is about transforming ourselves on the physical level and by doing so, we learn to ignite the original, innate wisdom mind. The fire that we generate in the body through tummo practice literally ignites the wisdom mind, which is inherent within us. Instead of only using the mind and different kinds of meditation practice, working with our different mental states, and so forth, by using our own body, and by generating this heat, we can ignite the luminous mind, the mind of clear light, *ösel* as it is called in Tibetan.

Each of the Six Yoga practices are designed to ignite the clear light mind. It is done in different ways, sometimes using the mind, sometimes using the body. With tummo practice, we use the subtle body as opposed to the gross body. A distinction is made between the gross and subtle body. There will be further detail about this later in the book. For now we just need to keep in mind that it is a form of going into ecstasy. It is a way to go deeper into yourself so that you forget your body shape and appearance and other predetermined perspectives.

You go into yourself and visualize yourself in terms of your subtle body with the "nadis," "chakras," and "prana." To reiterate, "nadis" are the psychophysical energy pathways, "chakras" are the psychophysical energy centers that are located in your body, and "prana" is the subtle psychophysical energy that travels through the nadi system, the psychophysical energy pathways. Normally our psychophysical energies, the pranas—there are multiple pranas—are not processed properly. They are blocked. Because the pranas are blocked at different psychophysical energy centers, we go into depression, for example. Depression, according to these kinds of teachings, comes from blockages of our pranic movement.

Therefore, when the prana is unable to move through our body easily, the mind also gets blocked. We can get fixated, obsessed, clingy, and revisit our obsessions and opinions again and again. The same scenes are replayed over and over. This happens mentally because on the physical level, the energy movement in the body has become restricted, arrested, and blocked. Tummo practice is designed to facilitate the pranic movement. It is said that the different movements of the prana become diffused so the energy is lost or wasted. Through tummo practice, one is trying to regather that energy and rechannel it into one's central energy pathway, the central nadi. By doing this, one's mind becomes more focused and one is able to ignite the luminous mind, the mind of clear light.

Dream Yoga

The next practice, which I will discuss in more detail later in the book, is dream yoga. It is also a very important practice. With dream yoga, we use the mind more than the body, unlike tummo practice. This practice is about seeing the similarity between waking moments and sleep. That is the key to this practice. Ordinarily, we see "awake" and "asleep" so differently. When we have a dream, we say, "That was just a dream." When we are awake, we are invested in the realness of what happens to us. For example, if somebody says something nasty to us, we may think, "What a nasty character!" and then hang onto that.

We do not see that we do the same thing while dreaming. If a character in our dream says something nasty to us, we often respond in the same way as when awake. In our dreams, if somebody says something nasty to you, you do not think, "Ha! How funny! This is so funny!" You get mad in your dream. You can become outraged and enraged just like you would be in your waking moments. When we see that, we see how we construct our own reality. That is a central point to the practice. There is the external world that we interact with as well, of course. How we interact with the world has so much to do with what is going on inside us, more so than what is actually going on outside us. We can see that we bring what we dream about into the dream from our waking experiences. This is something that we may not often think about.

We dream different things and then experience them while awake and sometimes experience *déjà vu*. We actually bring into our waking lives what we dream about, and what we experience during our waking moments, we bring into our dream life. That is what we are trying to see in this practice. Dream yoga is about maintaining that awareness when we are transitioning from waking into the dream state and back again. That is how we learn to exercise the luminous mind, the mind of clear light. Three stages of sleep are referred to in the practice: the pre-dream stage, the stage of dreaming, and the post-dream state. There are other stages such as deep sleep, and so on. One is supposed to observe all these stages as one goes through these experiences.

Yoga of Clear Light

The yoga of clear light practice focuses on the nature of the mind more than what is going through one's mind, not getting caught up with the content of the mind or the states of the mind but rather, the nature of the mind—the nature of the mind being clear light.

Illusory Body Yoga

In illusory body yoga, like tummo, one is supposed to forget about what one is as a person—our age, race, bodily shape, and so on—and look at the body as it is. The body itself is a product of causes and conditions. Therefore, the body that we have is in reality, in a constant state of flux, always in a state of transition. We do not just *have* a body. We think, "I have this body." However, we can think differently: "My body being in a constant state of transition is an illusory body." "Illusory" does not mean it is illusory because it does not exist, but "illusory" meaning that our body is in a constant state of transition.

If we see our body in this way, we will have a better perception of it. That is a side effect, but still very important. One is not thinking: "This is my body. I *have* this, so I hate it or love it. I love it so much and I don't want it to change. I don't want to get any older," or "I hate myself and I want a new body." Just being with oneself and working with oneself in that way, one sees the body in a dynamic way. The body is dynamic. We do yoga and Tibetan yoga (Tib. *lus jong*) practice, precisely because of that, to bring that idea across: the integration of the body, making the best of the body that we have, and not thinking, "This body I have is *'the body.'*" Looking at the body from a subtler, more refined point of view is extremely important.

Lus jong, for example, is about the integration of the body, speech, and mind. Tibetan yoga is not like hatha yoga in that regard. Tibetan yoga is about the integration of the body, speech, and mind. Even the speech element is introduced. When you do pranayama, you may utter some seed syllable or something like that. You say: "AH AH AH" repeatedly or "HUM HUM HUM." Instead of breathing like you normally would, forceful breathing as you might do in standard pranayama, you use your vocal chords while doing pranayama so that the body, speech, and mind are integrated. You say, "HUM HUM HUM," you act crazy! Tibetan practices can be unnerving, that is why they are esoteric.

Transference of Consciousness

"Phowa" practice is transference of consciousness, which is practiced in order to learn how to die properly. Instead of thinking: "I'm going to die in a state of total passivity, with no voluntary control," it relates to actually being able to control one's death. You decide when the moment has come so you then eject your consciousness. When you think, "I'm really dying, there's no other option," you do phowa practice. You eject your consciousness. You feel a sense of control instead of thinking, "I'm at the mercy of everything else."

This is an extremely powerful practice and we do this while we are still alive. When we do the practice often without ejecting the consciousness, we can have some positive result. Associated experiences can occur such as the crown of the head becoming sensitive from the repeated practice of phowa. This is not an uncommon experience.

Bardo

The bardo aspect has to do with what happens after you die. Again, according to Tibetan Buddhism, it is all about control, in a manner of speaking. All Six Yogas are related to getting control of our lives and being in charge. That is really interesting considering that in Buddhism, we talk about selflessness, non-egoism, and so on. It refers to how we can take control of our life situations and experiences. Even when we die, we do not have to think, "Once I'm dead, that's it. What can I do after that?" We should not think like that because even after we are dead, in the bardo, the intermediate stage, we can steer the course of our post-mortem existence in the right direction.

Tibetan Buddhism covers everything. Even when you are dead, there is still something that you can do. You do not have to think, "I'm dead and this is it." You can still change the course of your next life, what is in store for you in terms of your future. This is extraordinary and extremely positive. Whether you believe in future lives or not, still, to think like this is very positive. Even if you die and believe there is no future life, still, dying with that kind of attitude of being able to direct your own future would mean you would die better than if you did not think like that. Thinking your life is governed by mysterious external forces and that you have no control may be a far more difficult state of mind to be in to manage the dying and post-mortem states.

If we can think, "It's not up to fate or God but it's up to me," this gives it a whole new perspective, color, and flavor. Normally, we may think it is up to fate or God that decides what we have been—if we have been good, we go to heaven, if not, we go to hell. Alternatively, we may think it is up to fate. Everything that is going to happen to you is going to happen no matter what you do. In Buddhism, we believe we can contribute to how things are going to unfold, in terms of our dying experience—what happens to us during and after our death. In Buddhism, we take these considerations very seriously. There are practices that involve the bardo as well.

So that gives a quick summary of the Six Yogas of Naropa, the four fundamental yogas and two supplementary yogas of phowa and bardo practice. In section two and three I am going explain what is more difficult within these practices. How to perform the practices is actually very simple in comparison to how to understand these practices. I will also include some detail on how to do the practices.

Chapter Eleven
Mystic Heat Yoga (Tummo)

Normally, we all want to take charge and have control over our lives, but how do we do that? We usually seek to achieve this through egoistic means, thinking, "If I look attractive and have a nice body, then I will be really good! I should get more degrees. If I have a PhD and I am called doctor, I will be somebody," et cetera. While such considerations have importance, fundamentally what counts according to these teachings is that working with the subtle body helps to gain control. One learns to work closely on an extremely subtle level so there is less worry about such matters as age, appearance, physicality, and status, et cetera. One can feel good in oneself while adopting a whole new persona in the form of a deity, god, or goddess within one's practice. We experience ourselves with the qualities and attributes of the deity at that time, allowing us to more easily see a greater potential within and freeing ourselves from a fixated and habituated sense of self, opening up new dimensions of self-understanding.

With the practice of tummo, one assumes oneself to be a deity, goddess, or god. Usually in tummo practice, we assume ourselves to be Vajrayogini,[43] a female deity or Chakrasamvara,[44] a male deity. You assume this whole new persona. Deity visualization is not just a cultural thing that when transported to a new culture has less meaning or relevance. The relationship to the deity crosses cultural borders. In tantric practice, we do not concern ourselves with whether we *are* actually Vajrayogini or Chakrasamvara. What matters is fully committing to being and feeling like Vajrayogini or Chakrasamvara. There is a huge difference between thinking, "Is Vajrayogini or Chakrasamvara real or not?" and thinking, "Can I actually feel like Vajrayogini or Chakrasamvara?" This is important because you are thinking about yourself as an idealized version. You think that you already possess all the attributes you would like. If you are thinking of yourself as "Jane" or "Bruce," you may consider that, "I'm Bruce" or "I'm Jane. I don't have those qualities. I don't possess them. This is ridiculous."

In Buddhism, we say that one can use imagination for the right reason. This is important. We use imagination all the time. We fantasize all the time but often for the wrong reasons. Why not use our imaginative capacity for something transformative? Imagining in the right manner will lead us to having a greater capacity for self-appreciation, self-acknowledgement, and self-recognition. This is what the tantric teachings are talking about when they say visualize yourself as Vajrayogini or Chakrasamvara. You feel like you are the goddess; you *are* Vajrayogini. You have to look at the attributes Vajrayogini possesses and think, "I possess these attributes and qualities too. That is me!" You become in touch with those qualities and attributes within yourself. Even on a mundane level, perhaps many become wealthy because they picture themselves in that way. That is a different set of circumstances of course, but perhaps it is something similar.

With tummo and all the other tantric practices being discussed, it may seem excessively abstract, as if moving outside ourselves or delving into the spiritual realm while having little to do with our daily experiences. In fact, it is the opposite. The Six Yogas actually address two things at once. One is how to integrate our normal experiences in terms of our emotions, feelings, thoughts, attitudes, and so forth. On one level, in Tantrism we are supposed to transform the five emotions into the five wisdoms. That is repeated over and over. We have to try to understand this and find its meaning. The other is to ignite wisdom mind, clear light mind, or luminosity through the use of tantric methods. These two go hand-in-hand in tantric practice. If we look at tummo or mystic heat yoga, in this practice, we are dealing with the body and one's daily experiences of emotions, feelings, and so forth. As we progress to the other practices, we continue to ignite the wisdom mind. These tantric practices are intended to help us both deal with our daily experiences of anger, lust, jealousy, pride, and ignorance and, simultaneously ignite our own true nature, the nature of clear light mind.

Tummo means "fierce" or "fierce one," "chandali" in Sanskrit, which means "fire." "Mo" in tummo indicates feminine. The reason why so much emphasis is given to this is because in Buddhism, it is said that we live in the world of desire. In Buddhist teachings, this world is called *kamadhatu*. "Kama" means "desire," just like *Kama Sutra*, so "kamadhatu" means "world of desire." This does not mean animals do not have desires, rather, it means that our desires can take on many different forms, characteristics, and shapes. We do not simply desire what other living creatures desire; we have additional desires such as fame. Human beings are likely the only beings that desire abstract things, not just objects that you can see, touch, smell, and so on. We desire all kinds of things that cannot be seen, tasted, or touched. We may desire God's love, for instance, or justice, rights, and so on. These are abstract concepts only human beings desire. You will not find these particular desires in an animal. It is called "kamadhatu" the "desire realm" in Buddhist literature. We might think of "desire" in a limited way, but in Buddhism, "desire" is used in a very broad sense. It covers all kinds of aspirations, things we strive for, goals that we set for ourselves, and so on. It refers to the human experience; it does not mean any kind of focus on being animalistic.

Desire is such an important aspect of us. That is why the practice of tummo is so important. It is said that desire is like a fire. Since it is already like a fire, we should try to ignite that fire in the proper manner. If we can manage to ignite that fire properly, we will be able to transform that desire, experience, and raging fire that stokes our restlessness. As human beings, we are restless and harbor feelings of dissatisfaction. Desire and dissatisfaction go together and restlessness and dissatisfaction also go together. We are constantly dissatisfied, restless, searching for something, and wanting something. Therefore, we should go out of our way to ignite that fire and not try to douse it. If we do this properly, we will be transformed.

As human beings, sexuality plays a very important role in terms of how we express our desires. Sometimes what we think of as not being sexual is sexual. It is disguised and can manifest in other ways. From the perspective of the Buddhist teachings, such recognition is important. Tummo practice, mystic heat yoga, concerns feeling the sexual energy from just below the navel. This is also part of the practice of *karmamudra*, partnered tantric sex. It cannot be denied that the use of sexual energy is part of tummo practice. In terms of the tantric system, both karmamudra and tummo practice work with these energies.

There are four main chakras at the crown, throat, heart, and navel used in these tantric practices. In tummo, you generate and experience strong energy at the navel. Because of the prana or psychophysical energy (Tib. *lung*), we hold the energy there, not only due to our experiencing the energy. There are many different kinds of lung or prana, but at this point, you only have to understand two different kinds. One is the prana that arises from the lower part of our body and the other is the one that comes down from above. You need to think that this extremely powerful energy is percolating in the navel chakra.

We generate a great deal of heat so there is a lot of energy percolating in the navel center. In the crown center, the "male element" or "blissful center" resides and normally remains untapped. You do not normally experience bliss there until and unless the tummo or mystic heat is ignited in the abdomen. When you then ignite this mystic heat, the chakra in your crown opens and waves of bliss arise, in descending order and ascending order. First they go down through all the channels. The bindu, or the life essence, travels down and each time it hits the psychophysical energy centers, the chakras, you get waves of bliss. When it returns, you experience successive waves of bliss. That is what is described. The whole point of this is that normal pleasure and the satisfaction of desire are not comparable to the blissful experiences that you can have doing this.

The main point is about working with our desires without renouncing them, learning how to work with, become comfortable with, and being at ease with our desires. You have two choices. One is to say, "Desire is all bad. We should give it up," or we can say, "You can work with your desires. We don't have to give it up, but we will not be enslaved by it, beholden, or subject to any suffering that comes from having desires." In other words, we can desire things and when we get them, we are happy. When we do not get what we want, we are still happy. That is better than saying, "I wish I had it but I can't think like that. If I thought that way, it would be so sinful. I would be such a terrible person."

You desire what you desire but if you do not get it, that is okay. If you get it, then you are happy and everything is good. This is what tummo practice is about and why you do this kind of practice. You realize that you can generate bliss by yourself. You do not have to be reliant on someone to make you happy, to give you some pleasure, even on the physical level. It is a self-induced blissful state. You could be having a bad day, do this practice, and experience bliss.

Buddhism has always emphasized working with how our mind can change circumstances, situations, and environments. Tummo practice is no different. Doing this practice, even when our life is in a shambles, can put us in a totally different mental state. If it is done properly, it will not disturb our mind. Rather, we will be able to see things more clearly, what is good and working for us, and what is not.

We get confused when we do not have real bliss, when we have the fake, counterfeit version of bliss that we get from drinking, drugs, or having casual encounters with others. It distracts us. That is not bliss. When you experience real bliss, it clarifies the mind. It goes hand-in-hand with what in Buddhism is called "clear light." We should think of bliss and clear light as being inseparable. Real bliss comes with clear light. If you have the experience of clear light, your mind is clear, you are not confused or thinking, "This is so cool. This is so fantastic. I don't know what the heck is going on but I don't care." That is not a good state of mind to be in. Whenever we think we should have pleasure, it is when we do not want to think. We just want to blank out and pursue the pleasure, ecstasy, or whatever it is because thinking about it is too embarrassing or painful. It is important to know we can have real bliss and clarity of the mind.

Doing everything that we actually want to do without denying our pleasurable experiences, but doing them differently with the use of practices like tummo or chandali, is the key. We will then feel positive and energetic, feeling good without regretting having had pleasurable experiences. Whatever pleasurable experiences we have had will go toward making us better individuals. It says that spirituality and blissful experiences do not have to come into conflict. It is not the case that to be spiritual, you have to deny yourself pleasurable experiences. Just because you deny yourself pleasurable experiences does not mean you are a spiritual person.

If you read these teachings properly, you will understand that. This is what Tantrism is. As I mentioned, it is challenging. Tantrism is very provocative and may even be upsetting. This is the nature of the subject.

I translate tummo as "mystic heat yoga." Some translators use the words "inner heat." This is the most important practice of the Six Yogas. If you look at the Six Yogas practice as a set, then mystic heat yoga would serve as the foundation stone for all the other yogas to be built on. This is because with all the other yogas, like illusory body yoga, dream yoga, yoga of transference of consciousness, and so forth, it is assumed that you already have an understanding of the subtle body, how the nadis, chakras, bindus, and prana work together in harmony and how by working with these principles, you can transform yourself.

This is why tummo is usually introduced as being the most fundamental practice when it comes to the Six Yogas. You can do dream yoga and you may just be dreaming instead of doing dream yoga. It comes very easy to us, dreaming is not a difficult thing to do. Not only do we dream while we are sleeping, we are dreaming while we are awake. In essence, tummo is about generating bliss and clarity simultaneously. So often, when we gain pleasure, we get confused and there is often little or no clarity. Sometimes when we have clarity, we have no pleasure. We do not know how to connect the two: "How can I actually have pleasure *and* mental clarity for a change? Why is it that every time I find something pleasurable, my mind is confused and goes haywire and when my mind is really focused and on track, there is no pleasure? It is as boring as hell. Every day is the same." You think, "Is this what life is all about? What's this? This is not good or helpful." Whether you really admit it to yourself or not, this is truly our normal experience.

Tantrism tries to introduce us to this idea of how to bring pleasure and clarity together. That is why we speak about *mahasukha,* great bliss, and luminosity, ösel, the idea of mental clarity. These two can come together and that is what tummo practice does. That is what we are aiming for.

Psychophysical Energy Pathways

The nadi system should not be thought of as veins or something entirely physical. Rather, it is about imagining a kind of psychophysical conduit. The role of imagination is very important. We do not believe that the nadi system is something that can be found using scientific instruments. That is not the point. The important thing is that you feel it through the technique and this becomes a measure that the practice is working. It is what is important. How often do you feel something in your throat, chest, head, or abdomen and go to your local doctor and they cannot see anything? They say, "There's nothing wrong with you." They give you a clean bill of health. You walk away thinking, "Yes, I'm okay," but you do not feel okay. You do not feel well, you feel sick. You feel something in your chest, throat, or stomach. You have to understand the nadi, prana, and chakra system in that way. Sometimes health issues have to do with internal things that are almost imperceptible to the naked eye. Healing yourself is also part of this practice. Tummo practice is also about that. You tune into your own body, feel yourself, and see how you are going. You become in touch with your body and develop more insight into how to heal yourself. As I mentioned, it is also about being able to put yourself into a blissful state, in spite of all the things that are going on outside of you. The energy you generate in yourself is sufficient. You do not need more. With pranayama, you can generate to give yourself plentiful bliss and ecstasy.

Tummo practice is igniting the mystic heat in the abdominal area, and so much heat is generated in that region that it reaches the crown. This is true. I stated that it is the crown where the center of bliss resides. It is also said that this is male and the navel region is female. It is better not to become gender focused here. Basically, the only thing you have to know is that the fire ignited in the abdomen gains enough intensity to reach the crown chakra and access that blissful center. Then imagine, from having done this, that the bindu, also called bodhicitta, melts and travels down. Bodhicitta in Mahayana Buddhism, of course, means enlightened heart, compassion, but here it is compared to the seminal fluid of a male. There is this mixing of the two bindus, male and female. One gets a blissful experience when the two bindus connect. There is the female bindu residing in the abdominal region and the male bindu in the cortex. This is described clearly in tantric literature and this is so for all genders.

With the nadi system, three central nadis or energy pathways are spoken about; the right channel, the left channel, and the central channel. These three channels connect at each of the four chakras. This is why they are known as "channel knots." Due to this, the prana is unable to travel easily. It can be restricted. Different colors are also mentioned. The right channel is white, the left is red, and the central channel is blue. Even if you are doing tummo practice, this is not the most important thing. It is imagining that one has this energy conduit, almost like electricity. Imagining that is the key. If you think in that way, you will very likely experience the bliss and clarity being described. However getting bogged down in too much detail is not helpful.

Chapter Twelve
Illusory Body Yoga

Once you have practiced mystic heat yoga, illusory body yoga then becomes easier because you already know the nadi and chakra systems, and so on. "Illusory body" does not mean thinking that you do not exist. According to the teachings, it is not thinking about yourself in the negative or as if you are illusory. From a Buddhist perspective, that does not make sense. An example used in Tibetan and Indian logic to point out such erroneous thinking includes the "horns of a rabbit." Rabbits do not have horns. When you think of illusory body, do not think in the negative, saying, "It's illusory like the horns of a rabbit," as if the body does not exist.

It is said that when we look into reality, we can see many levels, from subtle to gross. When Buddhism was being taught in India, people did not generally understand it in this manner. Buddha and his subsequent followers realized that reality has many levels. It is not like saying, "God created the world." Buddhists do not think in that way. From a Buddhist point of view, reality exists due causes and conditions. There are gross and subtle levels. Such awareness is also shared by western science. If scientists look at a table, they will not merely see "the table." They will see its atomic structure, particles, subatomic particles, and so on. When Biologists look into your body, they do not see it simply in terms of your "body." They look at you in terms of your DNA, cells, and so on. They look at aspects of the subtle levels. All the levels are interconnected; the gross and the subtle levels are not separate. Illusory body yoga can be seen in that way. It is actually seeing ourselves in a subtler way than we are used to. We are accustomed to seeing ourselves the way we appear: "I'm a Tibetan and I'm five foot ten." We often see ourselves with a certain weight and so forth, but that is not "me."

As with the practice of tummo where we visualize ourselves as Vajrayogini or Chakrasamvara, similarly, thinking of ourselves more abstractly and generically can be very good for us and can make us feel better. Emotional and psychological problems can arise the more we concentrate on ourselves—how we look, what we are, and so on. If we go deeper and see ourselves in terms of our subtle body, we can be relieved of many of the pressures and burdens we place upon ourselves. With illusory body yoga, we can experience a real sense of freedom when seeing ourselves in a more subtle way. We need to understand that this awareness is very liberating.

To reiterate, "illusory" does not mean you do not exist. We do exist, but we do not exist in the way that we think we do. We exist on many different levels. This is also true on the psychological level and why psychologically, there are gross levels with regard to how our mind functions, such as our mental activities, and how we engage in the world. Sometimes it is very gross, sometimes very subtle, sometimes very inner, and sometimes it is secret.

In Buddhist Tantrism, we use these ideas, external, internal, and secret. These words apply to both the physical and mental spheres. Physically, there are the external, internal, and secret domains, and mentally also, there are the external, internal, and secret domains. In Tibetan, they are called, *chi* meaning "external," *nang* referring to "inner," and *sang* signifying "secret." We need to understand our physical and mental ways of being. The tantric practices can help us explore all the levels of what is gross, external, internal, and secret. Illusory body yoga is part of this process of discovery. For example, with illusory body yoga, our body as we see it is the external, but seeing our body in terms of the energy pathways, the psychophysical energy centers, and the life essence is the "inner" aspect. Following this, going deeper into ourselves and seeing how the body itself is permeated by luminosity and clear light is the innermost "secret" perspective. It is said in the tantric view that the body itself is illuminated.

When we do not recognize the many levels of our being, we can view ourselves with darkness and negativity and with endless limitations. When we experience the subtlest levels being described, our whole body should actually become radiant. This is why the Buddha is often described as radiant and having a golden hue. It does not mean that Buddha looked like he was made of gold, but if somebody were "radiant," that creates an exceptional presence. What does it mean to become radiant, irrespective of race, height, age, or attractiveness? When one develops such a depth of experience, understanding the chakra and nadi systems ignites the clear light mind. We can then realize that our own physicality is permeated by that light. We become a being of light. This is profound. When we are depressed, there is darkness surrounding us. When people want to engage with us, it may be difficult to find any lightness. When we are happy, even when a shyster dupes us, we are still radiating.

Tantrism explains how to use these experiences. It does not say that you can only have an experience such as this through Tantrism. Illuminating experiences can occur independently but we may not know what to do with them. Through the use of Tantrism, it provides the opportunity to understand such experiences and channel them properly, to use them in such a way that they become enriching and stabilizing. The illuminating experience becomes more real and integrated, rather than how it is normally related to. Even if we have good experiences and feel radiant, it can be very fleeting. The tantric practices can extend and stabilize experiences of radiance. With stability, radiance can increase in intensity, clarity, and occur with greater frequency.

Tantrism is not for everyone. It can be extremely challenging and provocative and one has to have an open mind. If your mind is not open, Tantrism may not be for you. Before you take on the tantric commitments, you have to decide to forgo many of your expectations. This is also part of the psychological and spiritual process that you will be going through with Tantra. It is not worthwhile embarking on these practices if you are resisting like a fourteen-year-old who is behaving like a five-year-old.

When a commitment to such practices is made, certain sacrifices are needed. When we have done something good in a non self-centered and non-selfish way, we may find that something good happens in our life, we may feel that we have done something worthwhile. Tantrism requires us to not only do something for others, but to also do something for ourselves. Self-sacrifice will be needed in order to get to the next level of awareness. It requires a strong commitment. For example, we know that we can feel good helping our grandparent cross the road if they are struggling. We think, "I've done something good!" and we both feel great. Tantrism is saying you can do something more. You are doing something for yourself but it is still a form of sacrifice. In Tantrism, the whole notion of sacrifice plays an extremely important role. In these practices, ritual fire pujas and similar practices may be performed, which are sacrificial acts. However, they are not like the monotheistic idea of sacrifice. We need to separate these two ideas. In monotheism, the sacrifice often involves a substitute. For example, Christians say Jesus died for us. In the Old Testament, God demands that Abraham sacrifice his son. We have this notion of self-sacrifice in religion and it is always about self, about our individuality, our relationship with others and our environment, and so on. In religious traditions, these stories are told over and over in many different ways.

In Tantrism, it is very different. You self-sacrifice, but you are doing it for yourself. That is the irony. The Buddha is not saying anything to you or saying you have to do certain things. Self-sacrifice occurs when one part of you dies and a new one is reborn. The old self is sacrificed so that the new one can begin to develop. As long as the old you is still acting out and behaving badly, then what you are within yourself, your true nature, the clear light mind, would have no chance to gain a footing or find habitation. Something that we are so familiar with in ourselves, that we do not like, has to die and then a new one will be reborn.

The Six Yogas of Naropa are designed for this. With a powerful practice like tummo, one needs to be open-minded. It is true that you induce blissful experiences within yourself and do not have to necessarily rely on others to have that experience, even on the physical level. You need to be very open-minded about these teachings. If you are not, then you are not going to truly comprehend some of the teachings. Instead, you may only receive a sanitized, watered-down version designed to avoid anyone getting upset. This is a concern because not everything that is unpleasant to us is bad for us. Equally, not everything that we find pleasant is good for us. It is important to think about that. In other words, everything that is challenging or difficult is not bad for us and not everything that comes easy to us is good for us. Sometimes we cannot handle a little bit of discomfort, but why should we not put up with some discomfort? Why should we not make some effort? Why not make some effort to make others feel better? This is what Tantrism is about.

I stated that illusory body yoga relates to going deeper and deeper into ourselves and forgetting what we are like as a person. Going deeper into ourselves may seem like losing ourselves, but that is the whole point. It relates to what I said in terms of self-sacrifice. If we do not think that we are losing something, we are not going to gain what it is that we want. Without loss, we cannot gain anything so therefore, first we must lose, and only then can we gain. So, first surrender. Once there is a sense of surrender, then there is the arising of a deeper sense of self-respect and self-enrichment. This is what illusory body yoga truly means. That is the illusory body. Illusory body is not, "I am thirty-four years of age, one hundred and eighty pounds in weight," et cetera. That is forgotten and you go deeper into yourself and then you see yourself as a body that is built totally of light and channels; the nadis, chakras, bindu, and so on. You have become this body of light and you think that you are radiant and enlightened. You think, "I'm an enlightened being, illuminated."

This realization is based on the idea that the gross physical body that we have is transient, non-substantial, and always in a state of flux, instead of thinking, "I have this body. This is so real. This is 'me.'" Instead, we think, "This body I have is illusory." As I mentioned, this does not mean it is like the "horns of a rabbit."

First, we have to understand it in terms of our own body not being different from our environment. This is explained in tantric literature and in this book. The literature also speaks about the microcosm and the macrocosm. Therefore, in the Tibetan Buddhist system, a lot of literature exists in terms of astrology, medicine, and so on. For one, the microcosm and the macrocosm correspond. We do not have to believe in astrology *per se*, but what is important to realize is that the microcosm and the macrocosm are, or should be, in harmony. With the use of tantric methods, we should learn to understand this. Tantric teachings often say we are not in harmony, and even though we are born into this world, we are not at home. We are not in sync with the environment and the world. In tantric literature, it says that our body is made up of the same things as the environment, the five elements: earth, wind, fire, space, and water.

This is extremely profound. Tantric psychology is built on this whole idea of synchronicity within ourselves, with and within in our environment. In Tantrism, earth, wind, fire, and so forth are not simply thought of in their grossest form. I referred to the idea of outer, inner, and secret levels of understanding. The grossest level of the five elements is that earth is earth, water is water, fire is fire, and so forth, but even in terms of our own body, we have heat indicating the fire element, our flesh indicating the earth element, our cavities in our body the space element, our breath the wind element, and so on. We might think this is primitive because the ancient Greeks spoke of this and we have now moved on and speak about DNA, etcetera. But there are more subtle levels than that. When we think of the elements, we might think of them as substances, but elements should be thought of as being dynamic forces that energize. They put energy into our lives and animate us.

Our moods, emotions, feelings, and physical states are dependent on how the elements are interacting with each other. If the elements are working together in harmony, we are more likely to feel positive and that things are working well. If they are not in harmony, we can feel depressed and low in energy et cetera. We may go to a doctor and they take our blood pressure, go through every test, and then give us a clean bill of health. However, simply because something cannot be detected with the use of scientific instruments does not mean things are not going on in the body. So the subtle body idea makes sense. The subtle body is about the elements, nadis, chakras, and bindu, the male and female life-essence. All of these play a significant role in terms of how we feel.

Sometimes people ask, "Does it mean that if you do these kinds of practices, you are going to be really healthy?" It does not necessarily mean that. If you attain clarity of mind and bliss, that does not mean you will not need a doctor. Your health may not be excellent, but you feel good and have a good attitude about life. You love and care about people and have a better attitude toward handling your unwellness. Equally, one can be in good health and be a miserable, whining, despicable human being full of complaints.

It does not mean that if you do these practices, you will not have any health issues whatsoever. It is about the attitude to your health, and how you relate to your mental and physical wellbeing. "Wellbeing" does not mean we are well all the time. "Wellbeing" means how you relate to your illness or how you relate to your "ill-being." You could be healthy and totally unhappy or you could be unhealthy and relate to it well, having a sense of bliss. Doing these exercises would help. People have reported normally experiencing pain, but when doing the practices, do not experience pain for the duration of that practice. So it can be like that even at a practical level.

If you do these exercises and induce these blissful experiences for yourself, then you are in bliss. That is one aspect. The other, to reiterate, is not about thinking that if you do this practice, you will become totally healthy and free of disease. That is not really the point. It is about realizing that you are free of disease on the subtler level but you may still have health issues on the gross level. That is a good way to look at it. Tantrism says this. In one's true nature, in terms of the subtler level of our being, there is no disease. On the gross level, it is true we will still have issues to deal with.

If we begin to think like this, our whole perception of illness, disease, how to handle it, and what we are going through will totally change. We might have been thinking, "I'm a diseased person" or "I have this issue," but it is about self-perception. In some ways, it goes back to what I mentioned in terms of self-surrender. The more we have surrendered that aspect of ourselves, the greater our ability to embrace the concept of not being diseased. It becomes much more of a reality.

To reiterate, with illusory body yoga, we should not be thinking nihilistically: "I'm just illusory, and not at all real!" Rather, illusory body yoga should be thought of in relation to the nadis, channels, chakras, and so forth. All are in interaction with each other so nothing is fixed. One relinquishes the whole normally held notion of our idea of ourselves as definitive, static, or fixed. That is the key to this practice. We actually do not relinquish the fixed idea of ourselves completely. We just have to demote it a little, giving it a smaller role than we normally do. The fixed sense of self is not put center stage in our minds. We let our mind continue in its normal manner: "I like to read this book," "I would like to take a walk," or "I like to spend time with this person." It only becomes a negative pursuit when that aspect of ourselves begins to take over and the inflated and highly fixed idea of oneself dominates.

Deflation of the self and inflation of the self also go together. From the Buddhist point of view, relinquishing the idea of ego does not make us become smaller. It makes us become bigger. All the Six Yogas are about gaining more control of our lives through the tantric practices. You have to be open-minded. For example, as human beings we have overwhelming sexual desires, so through tummo practice, we try to gain control over that. With illusory body yoga, we get distracted all the time with what we see, smell, taste, and touch, with all the sensory inputs. We think of them as supplying correct information regarding what is out there, objectively existing. When we dream, we believe in the dreams and everything that happens to us. While we are dreaming, we do not think of them as dreams so we try to get a handle on that with dream yoga. With transference of consciousness at the time of death, we are dying but we do not let our physiological processes gain the upper hand. We try to project our consciousness at the time of death to a higher level. In the bardo, the intermediate stage, instead of wandering around helplessly in a state of confusion, we try to direct our future course in terms of the assumption of a new rebirth, a new embodiment.

In that way, deflation of ego goes hand-in-hand with the inflation of one's personhood. In Buddhism, we do not use the word "self," but "elevated being," *phagpa* in Tibetan or *aryan* in Sanskrit. One becomes an elevated being by doing these forms of practice and it is the phagpa, or aryan who can guide their life. When we are egotistical, selfish, and self-centered, our lives are not guided by us. Even though we may be thinking, "I am doing it. This is me," it is not us. If we go down that path, that means ego, egoistic needs, will be satisfied. This does not mean ego has to be totally starved out, as is commonly believed. Ego has its own function and role to play; it does not necessarily have to cease to exist. Sometimes people may believe ego has to be starved out or rendered incompetent. The ego has its own role, albeit a minor one, and then you work together in a sense. We do not need to disable the ego functionality because it does not need to be fixed, but is malleable. We already have many identities: when we are with our parents, we project one persona. With friends, we project another. We are playing the role of a teacher, student, wife, husband, or partner, and so on. There are probably many more versions of ourselves, and why not? Instead of thinking our ego is only "one person," it is okay to play these multiple roles without becoming fractured in terms of one's sense of self. Sometimes, playing all these roles can be tiring and confusing. We can begin to wonder who or what I am. It is incorrect to think that our range of personas, suited to different occasions and circumstances, define us, as if, "How I present, is who I am." We have many identities and the kinds of practice being discussed here can help us to understand that all these different aspects of ourselves come from one source.

Chapter Thirteen
Dream Yoga

In section three, we will discuss dream yoga in more depth, but I will discuss some key aspects here. In dream yoga, one tries not to distinguish waking hours from sleeping hours. Dream yoga teaches how to cross from one state to the other. The waking hours and the sleeping hours are not seen so differently. This does not mean they are exactly the same, that when we are awake, we are really dreaming or when we are dreaming, we are really awake. Dream yoga says that when we are dreaming, there is some reality to it, unlike what we normally think. We wake up and say, "I was just dreaming," and may give little or no credence to it.

If it is a nightmare we wish to forget or a wonderful dream we savor, we usually wake up and think, "That was just a dream," as if it were nothing. Buddhism has a different view. Whatever karmic imprints we have created produce these life experiences. While we are awake or dreaming, there is a reason we have these experiences. We do not simply have these experiences without any cause. We have them because the karmic imprints have been left in our *alayavijnana*,[45] or as it is translated, the storehouse consciousness. The reason waking experiences and dream experiences are so similar is because they have the same source. Because we are not educated in that way due to our dualistic way of thinking, we say the dream experiences belong to one form of reality or "irreality" and the waking hours belong to a different kind of reality that is really, truly real. That is, we feel our waking hour moments are to be taken seriously and our dreams can so often be disregarded.

What is being said here is that the karmic imprints determine what we experience and how we experience. That is why dream yoga is emphasized. When we practice dream yoga, we realize that it is not only through waking hours that we can practice mindfulness and awareness to truly see what we are doing and how we engage with the world and interact with people. Even when we are sleeping, we can introduce a sense of awareness. Being aware is not sufficient; we also have to bring the sense of our whole being there, which means the body and mind together. One of Tantrism's most important targets is the idea of bringing the body and mind together so even when we are dreaming, we should not think of it as purely mental. What we dream about and how we dream relates to our body and our subtle body.

If you have been doing illusory body yoga and tummo practice or mystic heat yoga, you would then be able to do dream yoga with greater ease. Dreaming does not simply occur in the mind, it also occurs because of our physical state. Whatever kind of physical state we are in will also play a contributory role in what kind of dreams we have.

One aspect of dream yoga practice that is emphasized is how to direct the dream experiences. We have the capacity to change our dreams. If you have a bad dream, you can turn it into a good one. If you have a good dream, you can and should actually try to turn it into a bad one in this practice. When one does this, one realizes that this can also be done in the same way in our waking hours. We can put ourselves into different a mental state or mood through using our thought processes. Even in dream, we can start to think in a different way and generate diverse emotions, feelings, attitudes, and modes of being. One can also generate a sense of having a subtle body and go more deeply into that.

The second aspect is recognizing dreams as dreams. Even in

western psychological literature, lucid dreaming or recognizing your dreams while you are dreaming is discussed. When we are able to do this, we are not taken away by our dreams because we know we are dreaming. This realization is an extremely important part of the practice. In this instance, we do not have to see the dream as totally unreal, "It's just a dream," whereas when awake thinking, "That's reality." Rather, we can see the dream *has* a form of reality, and is not entirely separate from being awake.

In Tantrism, it is said that certain karma is being processed. If we are aware while we are dreaming, if we handle it properly, all kinds of karma are being processed. We become relieved of varieties of burdens and karmic baggage that we have been carrying around for a very long time. Of course, if Buddhism is to be believed, we have been carrying this around prenatally and also for many lifetimes before that. Whether this is true or not, it is still an extremely powerful way to relieve ourselves of guilt, shame, and many things that afflict us emotionally on the level of feelings.

Therefore, dream is seen as a form of reality and waking a form of dream. When we are awake, we are often actually dreaming and when we are asleep, we can be aware and wakeful. In deep sleep, we are not dreaming. With dream yoga, when we are awake, we have to ask, "Am I *really* awake? Can I trust what I see, smell, taste, touch, even on the sensory level? Is what I'm looking at and what I'm making of it true? When I see somebody angry, is that person angry or am I just thinking, "This person is angry"? When I think this person is amorous with me, am I just making it up or are they really amorous? I am using these examples because whenever we see, feel, taste, smell, or touch something, our mind can be so creative. Mind is the naughtiest thing of all, running all over the place. It is a wild elephant. You want to rein in the mind, but it so often refuses. Sometimes we can feel it is a hopeless situation as if our mind has the potential to ruin our lives.

When we are awake, we are dreaming of everything: a fancy house, car, yacht, and good-looking partner. We are dreaming, but at the same time, we are not dreaming. When you have your head on the pillow, you are dreaming, but there is a reality attached to it. When we are awake, when can think we are not dreaming. Our "awake time" is not totally made of dreams, but when we lose a dream we have held onto for a long time, we can feel destroyed.

This is the most authentic way to look at dream yoga. Instead of thinking, "This is all reality" or alternatively, "That was a total dream," it is all reality and dream at the same time. Reality and dream are not separate. It is part dream, part real. Because we have been conditioned to think something has to be completely like a dream or completely real, that can be so disturbing to us at times, even sometimes leaving us with a feeling of desperation. Dream yoga does not mean everything is a dream, but as I have stated, that reality and dream are not as separate as we assume. When we are dreaming, there is a reality attached to our experiences and when we are awake, there is an element of dream attached to that. We normally think they are so different. We often take events so definitively not seeing them as a dream. We can think, "This is the reality. This is the beginning of my joyful life," or "I'm never going to be happy ever again."

When we are dreaming and not consciously looking at our dreams, our dream experiences can be somewhat wasted. They can even reinforce our karmic imprints, making our samsaric attitudes and propensities reinforced, spilling into our waking hours. Buddhism teaches that if we do not process our karmic imprints, our unhappiness will likely increase and we can develop a tendency to attract negativity. For example, if we feel down, we may attract others who are also feeling down. If we can remain conscious and "snap out of it," even within a dream, we have increased our opportunities to change our negative mental states and begin to be and attract more positivity.

Buddhism does not say anything about not wanting to have good opportunities for oneself. We should seek good human relationships, job opportunities, and so on. While we are awake, because we can see the dream-like quality in life, we can dance and work with things. Then when circumstances change for good or bad, we have some understanding of what is happening. Instead of taking it too personally, and as being so real, we can see that it has pliability and can be worked with. It becomes another phase, another event in life. With such an attitude, we can have more of a handle on life and situations as they arise.

To reiterate, the Six Yogas are about getting a handle on our life, taking control, the inflation of personhood, and the deflation of egoistic identity. We ordinarily think the egoistic identity is what it is all about. The stronger the egoistic identity predominates, the less we can think of the sleeping state as wakeful and the wakeful state as dream-like. When we are awake, we need to know we are also dreaming. When we are dreaming, we need to know, "I'm awake and I'm dreaming." That way, we can process things more effectively. We can take control. It is inflation of personhood; we are not trying to become nothing or nobody. That is why these practices are so profound and beneficial.

Moving from one state to the other becomes easier because we see that they are not so different. When we are sleeping and dreaming or when we are awake, they are not so very different. As I said, this does not mean we think of them as being identical. It is "dream-like," *milam tabu*[46] in Tibetan. This is a deeply profound and useful way of looking at it. People often think that dream yoga means that one should view everything as illusory. People also think like that in relation to illusory body yoga, but that is not the case.

Chapter Fourteen

Clear Light Yoga, Yoga of Bardo, and Transference of Consciousness

The practices of the Six Yogas are quite straightforward; one simply follows the instructions. Of course, unless you have received the necessary empowerments and oral transmissions, you cannot do these practices fully. Through the instructions I am presenting here, you are receiving many of the teachings on how to perform and relate to the practices.

Visualizations vary from one tradition to another and also one technique to another. Such variations will not be discussed here. Tibetan rituals are also performed in a variety of ways. We should avoid getting too bogged down in these elements or ask endless questions about the practices. Instead, once we have an idea of what to do, we can simply begin. Many of these practices are about getting in touch with ourselves, learning about our body-mind complex. When we know how our body works, then we can begin to work it out for ourselves. When we know the technique and are using it appropriately to come more in touch with ourselves, then we are doing the practice very well. If we only think about the technique, then we will not be able to do the practice properly. Many people believe it has to be so precise, but what does that mean? "Precise," in what sense? Therefore, if we have the technique and we use it to come in touch with ourselves, then we come to rely more and more on our innate ability. Tantric yoga is about the internal aspect, not so much in relation to the external. With the internal, we should not get too fixated on the visualizations and so forth, because different systems have different visualizations, and we need to remain flexible and pliable.

With all the Six Yogas, and this is an extraordinary point about Tantrism, especially tantric practices like these, there is the idea of how to go into some form of amnesia and also attain clear light mind. In Tantrism, with all these practices, this is known as the fulfillment stage. As I mentioned, Tantrism has two levels, the development stage and the fulfillment stage. The Six Yogas are concerned with the fulfillment stage of tantric practice, esoteric practice. If you are doing Tara or Chenrezig puja for example, you are doing a development stage practice. If you do the Six Yogas type of meditation, esoteric practices, then you are doing a fulfillment stage practice. All the fulfillment stage practices emphasize the notion of dissolution and what are known as "empties," which I mentioned in section one.

"Dissolution" means the dissolution of the elements, the five elements of earth, wind, fire, space, and water. The elements are active energies, as opposed to something like truly material substances. Every time we do illusory body yoga, dream yoga, clear light yoga, the yoga of bardo, and the yoga of the transference of consciousness, we are learning to dissolve the elements. This is called the dissolution of the elements.

This is activated by working with the subtle body. With each practice, we are trying to make the prana enter into the central energy pathway and thus induce the dissolution of the elements. In Buddhism, we talk about emptiness, empty, and the same word is used in Tibetan, "stongs pa,"[47] but this does not mean we are realizing emptiness. It means that due to the dissolution of the elements, we are put into varying levels of the absorptive state. Our gross mental functions basically become disabled. Our worries, anxieties, and excessive conceptualization that we are constantly engaged in, all slow down until we are left with nothing but the clear light of the mind.

Clear Light Yoga

The practice of ösel, yoga of clear light is also about slowing down our excessive conceptualizations. Tummo is at the foundation, and illusory body yoga, dream yoga, and ösel, the yoga of clear light, are all interrelated. We try to realize clear light through different means, sometimes during the day, sometimes at night. It is very similar to dream yoga because dream yoga and clear light yoga are intimately related. Seeing the non-separation of being awake and dreaming, and using dream experiences to activate our mind to have full presence is what we do in clear light yoga as well.

In clear light yoga, it is accentuated, brought to another level. To bring about this understanding, we use different techniques when we are awake and while sleeping. For example, sometimes the practice of what is called "dark retreat" is used, which means we can practice in the dark for a short while. After that, we create an opening and let in a shaft of light. A mirror can then be placed to enhance the shaft of light. Different techniques like that are used at different times of the day and night. There are a series of visualizations, mainly involving the subtle body. In this process, we focus and rely on our subtle body, forgetting our normal form, and visualize a form of light, normally in the heart chakra.

When you are doing these varieties of practices, it is best to focus more on the lower chakra meaning, the point just below the navel. That is best because if you put too much focus on the heart or throat chakra, you can suffer from what we call "lung" in Tibetan. Sometimes people who do meditation sometimes end up suffering from "lung" from time to time, which means disturbance of the prana. Even when we are doing normal meditation, it is best to focus more in the abdominal region than the chest.

Basically, the clear light is induced through the movement of the two pranas, the rising prana from below and the descending prana from above. When they are pressed together, the advanced practitioner goes through the dissolution stages of earth, fire, wind, water, and space. According to tantric teachings, space is always at the end, which corresponds to the death process. So we are induced into the clear light state in that way.

In the clear light state, all the gross mental activities come to rest and there is nothing left but the clear light of mind—mind which is very lucid, clear, but not caught up with all daily worries, anxieties, or engaging with any kind of mental object. There can be a mental object but the mind does not engage with it. It is like a state of complete non-duality. It is described as a total experience of bliss and luminosity. That is clear light yoga in essence, ösel, which is intimately related to bardo yoga, because we go through these same processes at the time of death.

Yoga of Bardo

"Bardo" means intermediate stage. Our birth and death moments are separated and the gap between the two is called "bardo." Then there is the bardo that we experience at the moment of death and the bardo that we experience between death and rebirth. If we have been practicing tummo, illusory body yoga, dream yoga, and the yoga of luminosity, we would be extremely well prepared for dying. At the time of death, we would know precisely what is going on because even the moments of dream are seen as a quasi-death state. That is why they are so interrelated. When we go to sleep, the process that we go through in terms of body-mind, bodily states, and mental states, is like a miniature death, and waking up is like coming back to life.

If we have been training ourselves in that way, then when the moment of death arrives, we are already prepared because we are familiar with the whole process. We know what is going on, physically and mentally. We also learn how to maintain that sense of clarity of mind. Some form of amnesia may happen because we are not thinking about normal things, but there is such lucidity and clarity in the mind, which relates to our real self, our real nature. That puts us in good stead in terms of taking on the journey that is ahead of us. This is what bardo teachings teach and that is what we should be thinking about with the Six Yogas. With the bardo of dying, you go through the dissolutions and the four "empties."

The difference between the yogas—illusory body, dream, clear light, and the yoga of bardo is that the yoga of bardo occurs automatically. We can try to simulate bardo while we are still alive. It is called the "bardo of dying," as you create a similar experience to doing dream, illusory body, clear light yoga, et cetera. The whole point of bardo yoga is bringing the prana into the central channel and subsequently, the two upward and downward moving winds or pranas coming together. The two psychophysical energies press together and you go into that state of "absorption." Then you should have the experience of mental clarity. It is said that we would automatically have that experience of clear light, but we do not often recognize it.

When we die, the dissolutions are taking place and we have the experience of clear light, but we do not recognize it. If we have been doing all these forms of tantric practice, when we die, we can recognize clear light more easily because we have visualized it so many times it becomes familiar. We realize what is happening. Even if we are unable to recognize it very well, it is said that we might go into the bardo state and have all kinds of experiences in this intermediate state: first, not all that unpleasant, followed by very unpleasant experiences, similar to hallucinations. It is important that we recognize what is going on and see the manifestations as being manifestations of our own mind and not actual external beings trying to disturb us. That is the key. If we have been doing dream yoga, this would come in extremely handy because you experience these apparitions just like a dream. It is said you have interactions with the apparitions, which are sometimes pleasant and sometimes not at all pleasant. It can be very disturbing but if one has been doing dream yoga practice, one has some kind of handle on it and the bardo would be very familiar.

To reiterate, it is a way of gaining control over one's mental life and the different mental states that we may undergo at any given time. In other words, we are never at the mercy of external circumstances and situations. We assume rebirth and that we may be still alive in a manner of speaking in a post-mortem state, and in the notion of the survival of death. It is best not to discount these possibilities. Tantric Buddhism offers help even in times where we would normally be thinking it is beyond our control and fate takes over. Unlike theistic religious traditions where we may want to leave everything to an almighty creator, as practicing Buddhists, we believe we can do something. We are not only calling out to the buddhas and bodhisattvas, but in addition, we are thinking, "There's still something I can do! I remember doing dream yoga. This is like dream yoga practice, so I do not need to be frightened or feel lost." We seek to find that moment to experience clear light and mental clarity. It is said that we can then actually become enlightened during that state. We have the opportunity to become enlightened at the moment of death and during bardo. If for some reason we did not manage to become enlightened during bardo, we should not be thinking that we lost the opportunity to do so because at the moment of rebirth, we may not become enlightened but we could choose our rebirth, for example, choosing our parents and where we are born. Things of that nature are emphasized.

We need to exercise open-mindedness about these topics, but you do not have to believe in rebirth or the results of practice to do the Six Yogas. Often, we are so conscious of and concerned about all possibilities in life and death, we want to cover all the bases. If you have this training and experience, you would be better off than if you did not. I think there is a lot of merit in thinking in that way. Why is it okay to think like that while we are still alive and not okay when we are dead? It does not make sense. When we are about to take birth, we will have a better chance of choosing a better rebirth rather than a bad one. It is said that bardo beings have an element of what you might call "psychic powers," so they see their future parents and so on. But if strong emotions get the better of them, they will be drawn into taking rebirth in a lower form of existence. If their mind is not overwhelmed by strong emotions, they will find a better rebirth.

Transference of Consciousness

Transference of consciousness is the last yoga to be discussed in this section. This is practiced while alive and at the time of death. I have to explain this carefully so it is not misunderstood. It is a practice designed to help us have a conscious death that is not left up to fate or nature.

Going through the whole process of dissolution and so forth at the time of death, in the dying process, one ejects one's consciousness through the central channel and out through the crown. In that way, the practitioner leaves the body. It is said that the consciousness is able to leave through any of the bodily apertures. If it leaves through any other aperture of the body other than the crown, an individual may leave in a more confused manner. If one ejects the consciousness through the head chakra, through the brain, one is able to eject oneself into a better state.

The transference of consciousness or phowa in Tibetan is about remaining conscious so that one retains a degree of control and does not leave everything up to external circumstances. One is trying to gather one's thoughts, have presence of mind, and focus with strong aspiration. In Buddhism, we think of aspiration as being powerful. You gather all of your positive thoughts, emotions, feelings, and so on and then you roll all of these things into a huge ball. You are imagining it, and you project that into the future saying, "With this power, may I be born in good circumstances." You want to think of the best scenario. In this particular instance, it does not only mean having wealth and being born in a privileged environment. You may also wish for that, but most importantly, you think, "May I be born in such a way that I will be of benefit to others. May I have a great impact on others. May my next life be full of enrichment and of benefit to great numbers of beings." At the time of death, with these thoughts, one then does phowa.

SECTION THREE

Dream Yoga

Chapter Fifteen
Illusion and Reality

In some ways, this is quite an advanced topic. In other ways, it is not so advanced or esoteric because Buddhism has always emphasized the notion of the interplay between fact and fiction and reality and "irreality." I will elaborate on this notion as we progress. In the following chapters, I will first provide introductory remarks about dream yoga, then focus on the philosophy, and subsequently speak about the practice. I will discuss it in such a manner that I am not giving away secrets, but on the other hand, I will make sure that you understand what dream yoga practice involves and what the philosophy is about.

Dream yoga is not a subject Theravada or Zen Buddhists speak about. It is something that Tibetan Buddhists focus on. Within Tibetan Buddhism, it is the Kagyu and Nyingma practitioners who focus more on this type of practice than the other schools. The other Tibetan Buddhists schools also practice dream yoga, but with less of an emphasis.

Dream yoga, was brought to Tibet from India by the lineage master, Marpa.[48] Buddhism was originally brought to Tibet in the early ninth century and was then wiped out around the time of the reigning king named Langdarma. Buddhism was then reintroduced to Tibet and Marpa played a very important part in this revival of Buddhism. One of the teachings that he brought back from India was dream yoga. In India, Marpa spent a great deal of time with wandering yogis learning about different kinds of esoteric practices such as dream, illusory body, and mystic heat yoga. If you want to imagine what a *siddha* might have been like, you can get a fairly good idea from modern-day *sadhus* in India. He brought these teachings back from India in the tenth century, approximately. It became very popular in a short period of time and many people began practicing these yogas.

At that time, they were not known as the "Six Yogas of Naropa." They were simply different kinds of yogas that could be learned in India. They came to be known as the "Six Yogas of Naropa" once these practices became established in Tibet and became formalized. Naropa was not the only one who was teaching these kinds of practices. There were other *mahasiddhas*, such as the *sadhus*, who were also doing these practices.

As we have discussed, dream yoga is based on a fundamental Buddhist belief. According to Buddhist teachings, we are habituated, accustomed to thinking that what is real and what is not real are so definite; it is objectively given. We may think, "My mind does not have any role at all in terms of determining what I am experiencing or perceiving because these things are simply present. What I see or experience is the reality." Buddhism says that this is not the case. What is "real" and what is "unreal" cannot be determined so easily. Based on this idea, we practice dream yoga to look at the idea that whatever we are experiencing in dreams is as real as what we experience while awake. In our waking hours, we smell, taste, and touch; we have all the sensory experiences and then conceptualize about all kinds of things. We subsequently have emotional responses to various situations.

In itself, that might not be seen as all that informative or radical, but Buddhism goes further. Our mind is always involved in determining what kinds of experiences we have, and our mind and body are also intimately related in this process. We cannot understand the practice of dream yoga if we cannot appreciate this notion that the mind and body are intimately related. This is because in Buddhism, we speak about many different levels of the mind. We have what we call gross levels of mind and subtle levels of mind. Corresponding to that, we have gross levels of the body and subtle levels of the body. By relating to the different aspects of the subtle body, corresponding to that, you have the subtle mind. So to be an effective dream yoga practitioner, we need to become more familiar with the subtle aspects of our physical body by integrating that with the subtle aspects of our mind.

When we have too many thoughts, worries, anxieties, expectations, and are caught up with different kinds of painful memories, we do not have the opportunity to get deeper into our subtle levels of the mind. When we go deeper into the subtle levels of the mind, we also get in touch with deeper aspects of our body. As we discussed, this is called prana, nadi, and chakra. When we learn to manage and relate to these subtle physical aspects, we can induce a deep state of presence, a kind of mental presence or pure awareness where we are not disturbed by worries and anxieties.

Dream yoga is designed to produce a state of mind that helps us go deeply into ourselves, not just mentally, but also physically. It is a meditational practice that brings body and mind together. When we get in touch with the subtle aspect of our body, we can practice dream yoga. Dream, mystic heat, and illusory body yogas are all based on that same notion. This is a unique aspect of tantric practices: to use the body and mind together to access the state of pure awareness.

One uses the body in meditation to be aware and present. How does one do this? In brief, tantric practice involves the use of imagination. This is explained more fully later in this section. When we worry, anticipate, and remember things, we use images. Image is so powerful that whatever image comes to our minds, it arouses our emotions, feelings, and passions. We can see this in the use of advertisements that play on this notion. It is the same in Buddhist Tantrism. Sometimes people say, "Buddhism talks about chakras and nadis, the subtle body, but I cannot see it," or "There is no scientific evidence for that," but that is not the point. It is the imaginary body, which, according to Buddhism, has reality. Even if it is imaginary, it is real because, as I mentioned, what is real and what is imagined are also not something that we can steadfastly demarcate, saying, "This is the imaginary world and this is the real world."

What *is* the "real" world? What *is* the "imaginary" world? What some individuals may think of as being real due to their cultural or even personal background is also based on imagination; it all depends on what one imagines. In Buddhism, what we imagine to be true and what really is true are elusive and not something that we can put too much faith in. Thus, the tantrika sustains the idea that what we consider to be real has dream-like qualities. Ordinarily, we think that when we are awake, we are totally rational, fully functioning human beings and when we go to sleep, all these ridiculous images flood our consciousness. Dream yoga is a practice designed to teach us to think differently and realize that what we take to be so real is always subject to change. For example, what we thought was real when we were children and what we think of as being real as adults are very different and their reality reliant on our perspective.

The essential quality of a dream is its mutability. Anything can happen in a dream. All change is possible; a king can dream of being a penniless person, wandering in the streets, helpless. Conversely, a person who is penniless can dream about being a king and ruling with utmost power. Buddhism says that this is possible not only in dreams, but it also mirrors what we consider to be reality. With people in power, one day they are in power and the next, they are not. Someone who is not in power is put in power. You never know what is going to happen.

Dream yoga is about instilling this idea in our minds. The benefit of this is that when things change or do not work out, when they go weird, we do not freak out. We do not think, "My reality has crumbled. This is so terrible. I have no future." Dream yoga teachings are about saying, "It's a play." This word, in fact, is used again and again in the teachings. It is a play, a drama. Life is like a drama. It does not mean that we do not take any of it seriously. We take life seriously, but not too seriously, nor should we take ourselves too seriously. We can relate to ourselves and our opinions et cetera in a way that acknowledges the dream-like quality of how we relate to and apprehend the world.

When we are dreaming, the content of our dreams is significant at that time. Buddhism says we can actually create our own dreams while we are asleep, and direct our dreams in different directions. If we can develop that capacity, we can have more lucid dreams and even our waking hours can become more enjoyable. Normally, when we dream, we just dream and are not aware that we are dreaming. In the same way as when we are awake, when strong delusional forces are working in our heads, we are not aware. We believe the delusions to be reality. We can totally believe our deluded stories as if we have found the answer to managing our life and our problems. It could actually be the worst approach to take and yet with conviction, we follow our ideas convinced of their reality and effectiveness.

With dream yoga practice, we can change our dream patterns and recognize their dream-like quality in the same way that we wake up from delusory thoughts while awake. We can say to ourselves, "What was I thinking? Don't be stupid. This is ridiculous. This won't solve anything." When powerful images come into our minds while sleeping, we can initiate our waking up to become aware of our dreams. The dreams we have can become lucid. Instead of seeing them as real at the time, we can know while dreaming that we are dreaming. If one can do this while dreaming, according to dream yoga, we could also use this same method in everyday life. So the next time a person comes along on a white horse, you are not so impressed, thinking, "This is the best dream ever." You can still wish to go along with it, but at least you know it is a dream and not think, "Well, this is the answer to everything, all my problems."

This is the essence, the essential teaching of dream yoga, to learn how to recondition one's mind. Buddhism gives a lot of emphasis to conditioning the mind and it is explained in many different ways. One of the popular ones is called "mind training."[49] Almost all Buddhist practices are a form of mind training. Buddhism is about mind training because we have to recondition our mind. Unlike what some may believe, it is not about not conditioning the mind at all or being completely habit free. Only Buddha or an enlightened person can be habit free. Rather, it is about reconditioning.

We have been conditioned in the wrong manner for so long that we have to learn to recondition our mind. Thus far, we have been conditioned to be ignorant, delusional, and confused, so we have to recondition our mind to become more aware—to be aware and more cognizant of what is going on in our lives to take charge of our lives rather than letting our impulses get the better of us, realizing that even if we are not acting impulsively, our conduct may still be lacking. If we recondition our mind with awareness through the practice of dream yoga, for example, it would encourage us to be more spontaneous instead of acting habitually and impulsively. In Buddhism, spontaneity is equated with creativity of the body-mind complex and is seen as positive.

Dream yoga practice and other similar forms of practice allow us to recondition the mind. In Buddhism, it is not only while we are awake that we can use meditation to our advantage, but even while sleeping. Buddhism has something to offer us no matter what we are doing. The idea is that while sleeping, even if not every night, as often as possible, we can use that time for our own betterment. Sleep time and the time of death are considered, in Tibetan Buddhism, to be extremely potent moments. This is true in esoteric Buddhism generally, not only Tibetan Buddhism, because the mind has slowed down. In relation to gross and subtle levels of mind, in sleep and death, without actually practicing meditation, the mind automatically slows down.

When one is beginning to go to sleep or is dying, the mind becomes less and less active. This provides the individual with the opportunity to access the more rarefied and subtle levels of consciousness. These are levels that one would not be able to normally access when engaged in varieties of activities during the day. At night, if one can slow down and be aware of that aspect of the mind, one can experience greater depth than normal, deeper even than the formal practice of meditation. When one is awake, meditation may still be a struggle. However, if one can learn to go to sleep properly, one can learn to use that awareness in sleep and then go into a deeper state, into one's own being, which is otherwise denied to us while we are awake and going about our daily business.

Chapter Sixteen

Philosophy of Dream Yoga

In regard to the philosophy of the dream yoga, we first need to understand the relationship between appearance and reality. This is often spoken about in Buddhism: what is reality, what is appearance? In Tantrism, appearance and reality are not thought of as being totally separate. In tantric thought, the unity of appearance and reality is what is promoted. It is our dualistic mind that sees appearance and reality as separate, and reality as entirely external to us. Even if we do not feel we know what that reality is, we may still see it as external, standing apart from the appearance of the phenomenal world, our sense perceptions, and conceptualizations. There is separation: there is the reality out there that we are trying to understand, but the means we use to understand that reality is seen as something separate. Tantrism does not acknowledge that.

When we appreciate that concept, then we can see how using dreams might be helpful in terms of our waking experience. Otherwise, we are still going to be operating under the influence of our dualistic way of thinking that says, "When I'm awake, I'm rational, I use my thinking capacity, and when I am asleep, my thinking capacity is not there. I'm not as rational and the irrational impulses are going at full speed and I'm rendered helpless in terms of what images or other things might flood into my consciousness." Tantrism says that this is the kind of illusion that we live under and that is why, even while we are awake, we are having another kind of dream, a waking dream known as "samsaric vision."

Samsara essentially means "cyclic existence." Briefly, it basically means that how we experience things is repetitive and habituated. It is not only the pleasurable things that we experience that are repeated, time and time again, it is also the things we hate and truly despise. According to these kinds of teachings, that is a form of dream. It is not saying that it is not real. Of course, it has some reality, but it is not real to the extent that we think it is. No matter how many times we repeat something, it is never completely the same. Repetition does not make an experience of action the same. This is especially what is being taught in dream yoga. We may think, "I'm doing the same thing again. Here I go again," the same romantic interests, aspirations, and attempt to make our life meaningful. We believe we are doing the same things repeatedly but the "same thing" is not exactly the same. It is always different. Nothing can be repeated exactly. Samsara has that dual aspect. One is that repetitive nature and the other is the fact that the repetition is *not* the same. In samsara, we try to do the same thing again and again, hoping, "Last time it didn't work, but this time it should work."

It is said that the repetitive nature of our behavior and conditioning does not allow us to see things in a fresh light or to see the transiency, the dream-like quality of everything that we experience. Dream yoga practice is done in order to recondition our mind. Instead of trying to recondition our mind with the normal practice of meditation, the practice of mindfulness, awareness, and so on, dream yoga reconditions our mind from the unconscious, so that the unconscious has an effect on the conscious states.

Many Buddhist practices are about effecting change in the unconscious through the conscious. There has been much discussion of how the unconscious impacts on our waking state. Freudians and Jungians, for example, have a lot to say about how this occurs, especially in relation to dreams. Buddhism normally speaks about how to place imprints in the unconscious from the conscious states but with dream yoga, it is actually the opposite. With dream yoga, you are trying to plant seeds in the conscious state from the unconscious so that when we are awake, we will start to think and operate differently. This is why the notion of lucid dreaming is emphasized. We are trying to be aware even while we are unconscious. If we are awake, we will not be dreaming. If we are dreaming, that means we are not fully conscious. We are dreaming but we can learn to be awake, in a manner of speaking, while we are dreaming so that we can plant seeds in our consciousness, so that when we wake up, we begin to see things in a different way.

The most important benefit that is being sought after is not to see life in such a serious manner. Life can be taken too seriously, and we can tend to take every little irritating thing that happens in life to heart. We think, "This is just so unbelievable and terrible." However, in dream yoga, we can begin to see things in a different light so that when bad things happen to us, we are not affected in the same way. This does not mean that we are happy when bad things happen. That would be even more of a delusional state to be in than when we are unhappy. Realizing the illusory and dream-like qualities allows the seriousness we may place on our experiences to be eased. These seeds that are planted in our mind through doing dream yoga would then allow us to enjoy life more. It is not about seeing life as a dream so that life is seen as totally worthless. If we think, "Life is a dream and it's worthless," we are falling into the same dualistic way of thinking. Not seeing life as though it *is* a dream but rather *as* a dream allows us to enjoy life more because when good things happen to us, we can relate to that and accept it, and when bad things happen, we are more capable of dealing with the situation as it occurs. We do need to feel defeated or crushed. We should not feel like it has all been for nothing or a waste.

Several things are mentioned as far as the dreams themselves are concerned. The first point to be considered is that most dreams come from past experiences including past lives. This possibility should not to be ruled out. The idea of these past experiences possibly being like memories is emphasized in dream yoga literature. So we should think of dreams as reliving much of what has happened to us, in this and past lives. Of course, the dream itself is ornamented with present experiences overlaid onto one's past experiences. Even dreams about the future have their basis in past fears, unsatisfied desires, and expectations. Even if we are thinking, "I am living this kind of life in the future," that does not necessarily mean that one is having dreams about the future purely in terms of what life will be like. It still has to do with one's past experiences and is tied to one's individual karmic traces and dispositions.

The second point is interpretation of dreams to see if dreams have any significance. Once we have accepted the tantric notion of reality not being separate from one's own mind and mental events, and that appearance and reality are not to be separated, then, we can see the interrelationship between dreams and our samsaric tendencies. How we interpret dreams can inevitably change the reality of the dreams. Interpreting dreams is an art, not a pure science and there is no manual of dream interpretation in Buddhism that I am aware of. We cannot say, "If you dream this, it means that." Of course, we have a general rule that we use as a reference point to interpret dreams but how dreams are interpreted is dependent on the individual's capacity to understand the dreams. Otherwise, you gain from having some kind of general rule but you lose the richness in terms of individual understanding and individual appreciation of what one is experiencing. In other words, if two individuals have very similar dream experiences, it does not hold the same meaning for those two individuals. Just because a person dreams about a certain thing and subsequently mentions it to somebody, and that person thinks they have had the same or similar dream experience, it does not have the same meaning. It depends on the context so what one is going through at the time is significant. Trying to match one's own experience with some kind of formula homogenizes the outcome disengaging the art of interpretation.

With regard to the interpretation of dreams, as we are still developing as practitioners, we can venture a request to an appropriate lama to interpret their significance in terms of life decisions. To receive a meaningful interpretation from a dream, there is a custom to give a personal article to a lama. They then place it under their pillow or similar to provoke a dream that they will interpret for you to help you prepare for a major life event. This is something quite unique to Buddhism. You do not have the dream, the lama has the dream for you and then interprets it for you. This practice is quite common and is another way of using dream interpretation.

Another practice is that of high lamas such as His Holiness the Dalai Lama or His Holiness the Karmapa who may use dreams to recognize reincarnate lamas. Students or lamas may make a request regarding their master who has passed away and ask if they can find the incarnation. Instead of His Holiness the Dalai Lama or His Holiness the Karmapa telling them where the reincarnate lama will be born immediately, they would likely indicate that they would need some time to check their dreams. Based on their dreams, they may give instructions regarding whether the tulku has been reborn and where the reincarnation may be found. Dream interpretation is practiced in varieties of contexts and in many different ways. The proficiency is dependent on one's practice. We can trust such high lamas' interpretations due to their refined and practiced skills.

In Buddhism, it is not considered to be all that worthwhile to spend time on trying to understand what dreams mean. As ordinary people, we should pay attention to the dreams but avoid giving them too much attention or fixating on them. Instead, we need to do two main things: first, become aware of our dreams while we are asleep and dreaming, and secondly, endeavor to change our dreams. These two practices are related because if we become aware of our dreams while we are dreaming, our capacity to change our dreams would increase. If we can change a bad dream into a good one, we can wake up with a fresh attitude, be happier, more resilient, and positive. If we have not achieved that, if we have nightmares or uncomfortable dreams, we can wake up disturbed or sustain a bad attitude. Such days can be colored by our dreams.

Apart from the spiritual benefit, there are practical benefits to being aware of our dreams and being able to change them. This capacity allows more pliability during our waking hours as well. The main intention of these kinds of practices is to develop the ability to change difficult situations into positive ones in our waking hours. In Buddhism, waking hours and sleeping hours are related and not separate. Our dualistic mind says that when we are sleeping, *nothing* happens, it is just a dream, and while we are awake, it is totally real. We take this dichotomy so seriously and are totally fixated. There is no flexibility, letting go, or creativity. This total inflexibility can bog us down. If we look at things in a different manner, we can see they flow into each other: dream experiences, nighttime experiences, flow into daytime experiences and daytime experiences flow into nighttime experiences. They mutually impact on each other. Our conscious states and our unconscious states and our waking hours and our sleeping hours merge. They are interfused. This is the key point regarding the philosophy of dream yoga. Our inability to understand this is what causes us so much suffering and pain. Normally, we do not want to see it like that—

when we go to sleep, we simply go to sleep and if we have bad experiences at night, we normally just try to forget it or get over it.

Buddhism understands dreams in many different ways. There is not only one way to look at it. Even with dream interpretation, there is a sense of richness in terms of one's individual experiences as well as in relation to teachers or others who can interpret dreams. What is most important as part of dream yoga practice is the notion of becoming aware of one's dreams and then trying to change the dream experiences so that our capacity to change our conscious thoughts while awake is increased.

This may seem like a foreign idea, but the reason it is explained in this way is because sometimes our conscious state is its own worst enemy. When we are not so conscious, not thinking so much, and our mind is a little more settled, we have more capacity, not less. Again, our habituated way of thinking says, "When I am conscious, I have more willpower or capacity to initiate certain behaviors or actions," but in fact, when we are not worrying so much and preoccupied with too many things, that is when we become more effective. When we use the unconscious, the dream yoga practice, for example, we become more effective because we are not thinking in the normal manner at the conscious level.

In other words, to effect change, we have to use different aspects of the mind. When we are awake or conscious, we are familiar with certain aspects of the mind and when we are asleep, we are familiar with other aspects of it. Using those aspects that we are not so familiar with while we are awake can also bring about tremendous change in our way of thinking, even in terms of our conscious states. Bringing about some change in the undercurrent of our state of being is a very important part of this practice.

To reiterate, the fundamental principle of dream yoga rests on the understanding that the experiences of waking hours are not so very different from the hours of sleep; there is similarity. If we ignore that, we would be doing this at our peril because what happens in waking hours is not different from what happens when we are sleeping. There is interaction, some kind of confluence between the unconscious processes and the process of our conscious states. If we recognize this, we can become less divided within ourselves, overcoming many inner conflicts and unresolved issues.

Buddhism speaks about integration and non-duality. In one form or another, whenever we study Buddhist teachings, there is a continuous reference to integration and non-duality. That includes the integration of the conscious and the unconscious aspects of ourselves, of waking hours and sleeping hours, between our deeper self, our authentic individual self and our normal everyday life self, our persona.

Integration is an extremely important part of the Buddhist way of thinking. We want to bring all aspects of ourselves together so that we will not be self-divided within. If we are self-divided, there is a deeper wisdom we can listen to but instead, our tendency is to listen to and fixate on our own inner chatter. We can become obsessed and monofocal. In that way, our ability to appreciate life is diminished in proportion to our level of our fixation on our inner chatter.

We have forgotten about the dynamic quality and fluidity of life, and it becomes all about how things *should* be. If a person is not behaving the way we expect, this is a huge tragedy, so terrible. If we experience things that we do not like, we nurse that hurt, the deep feeling, and we will often not let go. Instead, we latch onto it and it becomes like a festering wound. The example of leprosy is used in Buddhist teachings; the more you scratch the wound, while there may be some immediate relief, the more it ultimately becomes worse. A lot of the things that we do in life are like that. Instead of looking for long-term solutions, we are looking at short-term solutions. In the short-term, we may get some satisfaction. It is like exacting revenge—somebody has killed your partner and you go out and kill that person. In the short-term, there is satisfaction but in the long-term, tremendous suffering has been created. This includes suffering for your family. There are consequences to one's actions that can negatively affect the quality of one's life.

Dream yoga practice is designed to help us to see the fluidity of life as an opportunity. It does not mean that because life is fluid, everything that we do is meaningless. Recognizing things to be impermanent, transient, and dream-like can help us to see life as providing tremendous opportunities. Just because we did things in the past that did not work, does not mean we are fated to failure and need to think, "Now this is the life I'm going to lead for the rest of my life." We may even think about this in terms of karma. Sometimes things have worked out but we do not want to acknowledge it or it is not completely to our liking, so that is not good enough. We do not appreciate it. Because we do not appreciate what has happened, we are miserable, unhappy, and want something different. We also paint a picture in our mind and think the picture has to fit our own reality, whatever that is. We think that tailoring reality to whatever picture we have painted in our mind will work.

Buddhism says we can see the picture in our mind's eye and reality as not being too different instead of seeing them as completely different. It may seem a contradiction but it is very important to develop this capacity. They are different when thinking dualistically in a dream-like state during waking hours. As I stated, when we are thinking dualistically, we are already dreaming even while awake, but when we stop thinking dualistically, we become more awake and we begin to see things in a different way. How do we experience this fundamental philosophical point in dream yoga? It is done by understanding how our mind or consciousness works.

In Buddhism, consciousness or mind is known as the "primary mind," and is described in many different ways. In teachings on dream yoga, we speak about eight forms of consciousness.

The first five consciousnesses are the sensory experiences through the senses: we see, hear, smell, taste, and touch. This is what we normally use.

The sixth is also called a "sense consciousness" because it follows the sensory experience. Our so-called "thinking mind" is the sixth consciousness. Our thoughts follow and are formed in relation to what we perceive through our senses—"I see this, I smell that," and so on. Everything that we experience leaves imprints on our consciousness.

The imprints cannot be left on the sixth consciousness or "thinking mind," to put it simply, because it is fleeting. It is a conscious state. Our thoughts normally go through our mind very quickly. I may have been thinking one thing minutes ago, and now I am thinking something else. Immediately after that, I will be thinking something different. Therefore, the imprints must be left somewhere else, but for the imprints to be owned, there has to be another agent. According to the dream yoga type of Buddhist psychology, the imprints that are left on this other level of consciousness, which I will come to in a moment, have to be owned by another agent.

The seventh is called the "egoistic mind." The "egoistic mind" says, "I am having a pleasurable experience or painful experience." "I like this." "I do not like that." Therefore, there is the egoic mind that synthesizes the disparate sensory experiences and conscious experiences, bringing them all together and says, "I am having this experience. That "I factor," is very prominent in how we own up to things, even those that we do not want to own up to. We unconsciously believe, "This is my experience. I experienced this."

The eighth is called the "storehouse consciousness," or alayavijnana in Sanskrit. It is also often translated as "fundamental consciousness." When this process is happening, these experiences can leave deep impressions or karmic imprints in the "storehouse consciousness" which is the equivalent of the western notion of the unconscious. It is called the "storehouse consciousness" because all these imprints collected in the course of our daily activities are stored there (Skt. *alayavijnana*; Tib. *kun gzhi rnam shes*).[50]

All of our dualistic ways of thinking come from the interaction of these different states of consciousness. In Buddhism therefore, we do not think of the mind or the body as just one thing. In many ways, we have minds rather than mind. Mind is like a corporation, there are many different departments and each department has its own function. When they are all working together, we could think of ourselves as having a sound mind. When they are not working together very well, we can have less of a sound mind. This is one of the most important insights that Buddhism has offered regarding the mind: that mind is not one singular thing but rather has many aspects. It is like functionalism's notion of the mind: mind has many different functions and if they all cooperate and work in unison, things can work out well. However, if they are not working in unison and are going in different directions, it does not work out so well.[51]

In Buddhist psychology, mental events are seen as having a separate operation. We have positive and negative mental events and these mental events, again, have to cooperate with the primary mind. The mental events relate to positive and negative thoughts and emotions, and so on. According to Buddhism, we get so troubled and confused when there is tension in the mind, with all of these interplays going on, because mind is not simple. If it were simple, we would not get confused or be self-divided. Due to mind being a "complex phenomenon," as Buddhists would call it, we can get confused.

Our Authentic State

When we have dreams, the karmic imprints that are planted in the storehouse consciousness reappear. Most dreams arise from the storehouse consciousness. We also have Buddha-nature or *tathagatagarbha* in Sanskrit. Many different words are used for Buddha-nature. Literature that discusses dream yoga refers to "clear light mind" which is similar to Buddha-nature. "Dharmakaya" is also sometimes used. These different terms can be considered as referring to the same thing, one's own authentic nature of being. "Buddha-nature," "Buddha mind," and "wisdom mind" are basically referring to one's own authentic state of selfhood as opposed to the egoic mind. We have some idea then, that our normal experience, which is very self-centered in the Buddhist sense, is limiting and causes suffering.

To be truly "self-centered," one has to access one's authentic state of being. Doing dream yoga allows us to do that; to find access to one's own authentic state of being so that whatever we are experiencing while dreaming does not leave karmic imprints in the storehouse consciousness where the delusory experiences will be repeated time and time again. In our normal state, whenever we experience something, the imprints are left in the storehouse consciousness and we then simply act impulsively, often without thinking. There is a difference between spontaneity and impulsive behavior. Due to being karmically conditioned, we may act out impulsively or habitually. It may seem like a spontaneous way of behaving, but it is not spontaneous because the karmic impulses have initiated that particular action. In contrast, if we have learned to access a deeper state of being, when one acts, instead of through impulse, one can respond with the truest spontaneity.

Dream yoga is designed to produce such a clear light mind because with this practice, we gradually learn to be in an authentic state. Then we can operate on that level instead of incessantly planting more karmic imprints. In the beginning, the idea is to plant positive karmic imprints in the mind and then gradually go beyond karmic imprinting. That is why we speak about the transformation of our dreams. I already stated that we may have a bad dream and can learn to change it so that it becomes a good dream. These good dreams then plant good seeds in the storehouse consciousness. This, in turn, will have an impact on our thinking mind and egoic mind. Even on the sensory level, we will also see and hear things in a different way.

According to Buddhism, buddhas do not have dreams, but I will leave that up to you to ponder. After we have practiced for a while, we may have less dreams. When we do dream, we can begin to receive dreams from a deeper state of being and selfhood, not just from our egoic identity or self-identification. Rather, it comes from something much deeper. These dreams hold much more significance to a Buddhist practitioner than the dreams that we receive from the storehouse consciousness, a product of karmic traces and dispositions. What is more important is having "luminous dreams," dreams that portend self-development.

Even if we believe we understand our dreams on a particular level, this does not necessarily mean we are developing as a person. Just like in waking hours, simply because we understand that certain things are happening in our lives does not mean that we are becoming more intelligent or developing more rapidly than if we were not. Of course, it helps, but it does not necessarily mean we are *really* developing in a genuine sense. It is important to develop in a much more authentic way. If someone has annoyed you for example, and did so not only from your point of view, but you also looked into their psyche or learned a little about why this person acted unpleasantly and you then found out that it was because they were jealous, simply knowing that in itself will not necessarily make you a better person. We have to learn from our experiences. If we learn to go deeper into ourselves, then even when we have dreams that arise from the level of the storehouse consciousness, we can use that to our advantage so that we can develop. It is important to develop a deeper understanding of dreams and learn to distinguish the helpful dreams from the ones that are not helpful. Then we can use the helpful dreams to our advantage for personal cultivation.

As part of the philosophy of dream yoga practice, we use different levels and aspects of consciousness—the eight forms of consciousness and this includes the body. The body should be understood in terms of three principles discussed throughout this book: the nadis, chakras, and prana. These three have to be harnessed so that we can go deeper into our authentic state of being instead of getting caught up in dualistic misperceptions and confusion. The three main nadis or psychophysical energy pathways: central, right, and left need to be aligned with the chakras or psychophysical energy centers in the body to integrate the nadis. Our minds can then be more settled and the tendency to engage in all kinds of discursive thoughts and emotions will reduce. Then one can experience real calmness enabling one to access the true original state of being.

Sleep and Dying

As I mentioned, going to sleep and dying are considered very similar. According to Buddhism, when we go to sleep, a similar process occurs to dying. In western literature, they have called sleep a "small death," so that idea is not foreign in the west. When one is practicing, this is also supposed to help the individual to prepare for one's death because the process is very similar such as the sense of loss of willpower and consciousness. If we become somewhat successful with doing dream yoga repeatedly, when we die, we will not see the process as foreign or unknown. We would not be at a total loss as would normally be the case. Normally when we go to sleep, we dream and have no control over whatever dreams we have.

If we practice dream yoga and learn to truly direct our mind while dreaming, even for a short time, it should help us at the time of death and in the post-mortem state. From the Buddhist perspective, in death, the visionary experiences and vision's dream-like qualities are recognized.

In *The Tibetan Book of the Dead*, it speaks about wrathful and peaceful deities appearing. Sometimes people may get fixated on the cultural aspect of these teachings, but all it means fundamentally is whether we are dying or going to sleep at night, similar things happen in our mind. Sometimes we have good, peaceful dreams and other times, we have bad ones. If we can deal with what is going on during our dream experiences, then when we are dying, we do not need to be frightened. We can use that time to our own advantage.

Whether we believe in rebirth or not, when we die, most of us will encounter many terrifying experiences and I am sure we would want to die peacefully rather than in terror. Just like going to sleep, we cannot simply say, "I don't believe in dreams. I don't believe in nightmares," and hope that just by thinking, "I don't believe in nightmares," that one will not experience them. It does not work like that. In the same way, just by saying, "When I die, I'm not going to have any unpleasant experiences," will not make the unpleasant experiences go away.

Fundamentally, dream yoga practice is designed to make us live well, but it is also designed to help us die well. If we live our life without too much fixation, obsession, worries, and anxieties, and be a little more relaxed and less rigid and uptight, we can enjoy life more. When the time to die comes, we can be prepared. When difficult situations arise such as a bad car accident, the idea is that dream yoga can help us deal with such difficulties. When we find ourselves in a difficult situation, we can be more prepared. Being able to remain connected with others even at the time of death is achievable and a wonderful alternative to collapsing into a state of unconsciousness.

Dream yoga helps to merge the outgoing forces of the consciousness with ingoing forces of consciousness. If we think of consciousness as a field, there are the psychic forces going outward, dispersing in the form of sensory impressions and egoic preoccupations, and there are also the forces that are actually there that draw things into the center. The concept of Buddha-nature or clear light mind draws things in to stabilize and awaken the mind. How far we move from that particular energy will determine how integrated we are as a person, our psychic integration. The more we move away from that and resist that pull, the more we become confused. If we can acknowledge the inward movement of that psychic pull, and work with outward movement, we can achieve integration of the two movements, one going in and one going out. It is lopsided if we are just going in one direction. Even if it is going inside, deeper and deeper into ourselves, we can lose sight of our sensory impressions, sensory experiences, ordinary life experiences, and so on. This can create separation rather than a sense of wholeness or balance.

Many people on a spiritual path may have focused on continually going deeper into oneself, feeling that going outward can disperse one's efforts and one can become lost in sensory impressions and egoic preoccupations, thinking, "Now I have to focus on following this path of 'mind of clear light.' I have to go into that one direction." Integrating the two directions is the optimum. Lucid dream practices build awareness of this balance.

Chapter Seventeen

The Practices of Dream Yoga

In the previous chapter, I discussed the philosophy of dream yoga, how to integrate it into everyday life, and how the practice of dream yoga should not be seen as a method of devaluing our everyday life experiences but rather, as a way of enhancing them. This is the case because we try to bring something that we learn from dream yoga practice into everyday life. What we do in everyday life, we can also bring into dream yoga practice and we can bring something that we have learned in dream yoga practice into everyday life.

I will not go into an extremely elaborate description of the practices, but I will provide much of the pith. Dream yoga practice is a very esoteric form of Tibetan Buddhist practice and in order to do it, you need to work with a particular teacher. You also need authorization, which in our tradition, is referred to as the receiving of the abisheka, empowerment or initiation. When I say I am not going to go into the details, I mean simply the aspect requiring permission, but I will nevertheless discuss the practice. One can perform this practice to a degree before receiving the necessary empowerments. It is advisable to make a start and then if you think it is the kind of practice you want to go further into, you can complete the necessary empowerments and instructions with your teacher or vajra master. One cannot just start practicing it fully. Making effort in that direction helps to develop an idea of the practice through personal experience, then one can see whether or not that practice is something one wishes to pursue seriously. Once you have made the full commitment, received the empowerments and the instructions, you are expected to continue. So it is good to experiment beforehand and try to become familiar with the teachings and practices so that you can decide whether it is something that you want to commit to fully or not. It is my hope that you think that this practice is helpful, useful, and something that you would like to go on with. I will now discuss the practical instructions.

Step One: Shamatha and Pranayama

When you do dream yoga at night, it is first advisable to do a shamatha type of meditation, calming meditation.[52] You calm your mind down. You do not have to sit for one or two hours or even do hours and hours of shamatha. Even if you do it for ten minutes, that is very helpful. If you do some pranayama or breathing exercises, which you can learn from yoga teachers, this is also very helpful. If you do not perform pranayama, you can simply breathe in and out with fairly vigorous breathing. You do that three or seven times. When you breathe out, you breathe out all your tension and when you breathe in, you try to feel your muscles relaxing and your chest, pelvis, and stomach relaxing. This is extremely helpful. Therefore, you can do that with shamatha meditation, combining pranayama with shamatha.

Step Two: Guru Yoga Prayer

Following this, according to traditional practice, you have to do some kind of guru yoga practice. In other words, you have to invoke powers outside of yourself. We do not have to think, "I have to do everything by myself," or "I have to find everything in myself." It is good to think of buddhas, bodhisattvas, and enlightened beings, and make supplication to them. One can do a simple form of guru yoga, making a small wishing prayer, saying, "Give me the strength so that I can do this practice and that when I am dreaming, I won't get sidetracked or lost. Keep me focused and please give me your blessings." This helps to put oneself in a proper frame of mind. If we invoke a sacred energy, we are able to feel that. If you think, "I'm just going to lie down and see what happens. I'll see how this thing works. I'll just try to watch my dreams," it is not going to work. One creates the atmosphere and then enters into that mental state. By doing this, one is leaving our mind state and creating a more appropriate frame of mind to succeed with this practice.

In other words, preparation is as important as the actual practice. Often, we do not spend enough time on the preparation; we just throw ourselves into something and then find that we are not ready to deal with whatever we have taken on. Spiritual practices, Buddhist practices, are no exception. If we do the preparations every time we do dream yoga practice, and also any other kind of practice, we will be served very well. This is a very important point.

Step Three: Posture and Breath

At this point, one can prepare to go to sleep. When you go to sleep, if you are male, you lie on your right side and if you are female, you lie on your left side. You do not have to be so strict about this necessarily, it is enough that you lie on your right or left side. As long as you are lying on your side, this should be sufficient. It is explained in this manner because, with the three energy pathways, the three central pathways (Skt. *nadi*) according to tantric esoteric teachings, males have a connection, something that they have to deal with regarding the right channel or right psychophysical energy pathway, and the females have a connection, something that they have to deal with regarding the left psychophysical energy pathway. While you are lying down on your left or right side, one part of the lung is compressed. It is also said of the breathing aspect regarding the use of the nostrils, if you are lying on your left, breathing through the right nostril is enhanced and if you are lying on your right, breathing through the left nostril is enhanced.

Breath is connected with the prana so if we are breathing in a proper fashion and holding the proper posture in that way, when you are resting on your left, you have your left hand resting under your head and the right hand resting on your hip. When you are lying on your right side, you should have the right hand under your head and have the left hand resting on your hip. You have the knees slightly bent, and this is emphasized because it will make it more comfortable to lie in that position instead of having one leg on top of the other with legs straight. You start in that posture and breathe normally.

Step Four: Visualization

Next comes visualization practice. As I mentioned, in esoteric Buddhist practices, we try to bring together the prana, the psychophysical energy or wind element, as it is sometimes translated, the nadis, the psychophysical energy pathways, and the chakras, the psychophysical energy centers. To do this, we also have to bring body and mind together. This will not just automatically happen. The nadis, prana, and so on will not just come into operation in a harmonious manner without the contribution of the mind. Therefore, you have to bring in visualization practice. You practice visualization in order to activate the prana and to ensure that the chakras and nadis are in alignment.

There are many different kinds of methods of visualization in Tibetan Buddhism but I will give one that is based on the Nyingma tradition. Here, you can visualize the syllable "AH."[53] In the Nyingma tradition, the letter "AH" has enormous significance. It is not simply a randomly chosen letter; "AH" represents ultimate reality. I discussed how appearance and reality are not separate and the letter "AH" is a symbol of that. Whether you visualize the letter

"AH" in its Tibetan, Sanskrit, or English form, it still has some kind of form attached to that, but in itself, it represents reality, emptiness, and the non-separability of appearance and reality. The point is that appearance and reality are not so very separate. This is an extremely important concept especially in Kagyu and Nyingma teachings: the unity, as it is described, of appearance and reality, (Tib. *snang stong zung 'jug*). [54] "Snang" means appearance, "stong" means emptiness, reality, and "zung 'jug" means coming together, so it means the coming together of appearance and reality. You could say that all of one's experience during sleep is the experience of that, of appearance and reality.

You start with the visualization of the letter "AH" in your heart chakra. It can be resting on a five petal lotus at the heart chakra. The idea here is a sense of opening up. Due to our fixations and obsessions, we have what are described as "knots" of the nadis at the chakra points. When we learn to integrate the prana, chakras, and nadis, the knots become loosened. It is like an opening up of the centers and releasing a great deal of psychophysical tension in the body.

As human beings, we are prone to using images, so in tantric Buddhism, it is said that we have to use images in order to enter an imageless or formless state. All tantric practices are about that. The development and fulfillment stages of practice are about this and it is the same in dream yoga. For instance, in the Nyingma tradition, they make a distinction between dream yoga and sleep yoga. In sleep yoga, there is no visualization and in dream yoga, you have visualization. In traditional tantric practices, when you do the practice of the *sampattikrama*, development stage, when you are doing visualization, you use images. When you do the Six Yogas, including dream yoga, one goes beyond images. The whole idea is to go beyond images but you use images to do that. That is why we do visualizations. Visualizing the letter "AH," for example, is a way to help us with that. The letter "AH" is white in color to represent our original purity, our wisdom mind, as I have been describing it, and what is also often called mind of clear light. Then we focus on the letter "AH," trying not to think about anything, trying to rest simply with that notion.

Step Five: Waking Up Through the Night

If one is doing dream yoga properly, the night is divided into different segments. You have the dusk, midnight, and dawn periods. You are supposed to wake up after two or three hours each time and then retrain yourself to go back to the practice rather than for example, starting the practice, becoming conked out, and subsequently waking up at eight o'clock in the morning. In order to train with the dream yoga practice, you go to sleep and do that for a period of time, two or three hours. You can use an alarm clock if you wish. Even if one does not want to do that, the point is that if one can learn to wake up at least once or twice after first falling asleep, it would help.

The next time you wake up after focusing on the "AH," to prevent yourself from going off on a tangent you could multiply the "AH" visualization. You visualize the first "AH" as before, then add a second, then a third—you multiply them and stack them up on top of each other in order to keep yourself occupied. This is seen as very important because we want relaxation so that we are not thinking, "I'm still awake. I can't go to sleep." On the other hand, we do not want to be so sleepy that we are unable to keep any kind of awareness as we drift off to sleep. Of course, as practitioners, we are not expected to stay awake all the time. The point is that if we learn to do this, there will be some kind of wakefulness that is maintained as we drift into sleep, which then might be used as a triggering mechanism that comes on when you start dreaming. You then become aware of your dreams.

The next time you wake up, to make it helpful, instead of going back to visualizing "AH," because you have already done so and your mind may be bored with that, you can visualize a lotus at the heart chakra and a luminous ball of light the size of a sesame seed, a tiny little bulb of light, and you focus your mind on that. You may have changed your position in your sleep, so you then reposition yourself and lie on your right or left side if possible or whatever is comfortable. Subsequently, you redo the same thing as earlier and try to go back to sleep.

When one wakes up again, it is said that you can change your lying position. You could prop yourself up comfortably in bed by stacking a few pillows or something similar. The legs can be slightly crossed, not in meditative position, but loosely crossed. It does not matter which foot is resting on the top or bottom, they are just resting like that. One then puts one's arm over the other arm with one hand on the forearm or wrist and the other hand against the body, loosely crossed over one's front near the heart or upper abdomen and goes to sleep. One again thinks about the practice, trying to remind oneself that, "I'm doing dream yoga practice," despite sleepiness or whatever the case may be, and then try to go to sleep with some sense of awareness. This concludes the description of the basic procedure of the practice.

Recognition, Transformation, and Liberation

What do we do with the dreams themselves? Many different things are mentioned but three things are important: recognition, transformation, and liberation. After doing these, we may start dreaming.

1. First we need to train ourselves to recognize our dreams, realizing, "I'm dreaming. I'm having such and such a dream." This can be hard to do, but it is the first step.

2. Secondly, after recognizing our dreams, we can then transform them. It is explained in this way: many dreams can be reduced

to one and one can be multiplied into many. Peaceful dreams can be turned into violent ones and violent ones can be turned into peaceful ones.

In the beginning, we just have to learn to recognize. It is the basic form of lucid dreaming. The second step is to transform, to change our dreams. This is seen as an extremely important practice, even though people sometimes do not appreciate the notion that we should change dreams while we are dreaming. We may think the unconscious carries messages and that if we change the dreams, we are depriving ourselves of understanding what the unconscious mind is trying to tell the conscious mind. We may believe that we would end up not learning anything about ourselves because we are trying to change our dreams. This is not the Buddhist view. As I mentioned in previous chapters, in Buddhism, we do not draw such a sharp and fast demarcation line between the unconscious and the conscious. There is continuous two-way traffic moving from the conscious influencing the unconscious and vice versa. Again, the Buddhist notion of non-duality is relevant, as we do not see the unconscious and the conscious as two totally separate realities. Our belief in this separation is another form of fixation. The notion of the unconscious or the conscious is a form of mental construct in a fundamental sense.

The dream experiences while one is dreaming can be brought into one's daily life to make one's life much more enjoyable and one can use one's own conscious states and take that into the dream state and then change one's dreaming patterns. Buddhist meditation practitioners who are experienced in how the dreams change over time have given guidance on managing dreams. With regard to transformation, two different kinds of dreams are spoken of. First, you deal with the more innocuous or less disturbing dreams and then you deal with the more disturbing ones. Next, you try to turn the peaceful ones into disturbing dreams and the disturbing ones into more peaceful ones. If we can do that, we can bring this into our daily life. When we have a bad experience in real life, during waking hours, we may then be able to change that into something constructive and helpful. The purpose of making good dreams into bad ones is that it is supposed to teach us that our mind does that all the time. It is supposed to teach us how our mind can create things. We get so fixated on what we believe is real, what we believe is not real, and that can color our whole worldview and how we experience everything. But reality is not so fixed. It is a very helpful lesson to see how very powerful our mind is.

Even without Buddhist training, we know that if we have the right approach, bad experiences can be used in a constructive manner in order to grow. Bad experiences do not necessarily have to be "bad." Many of the bad experiences are cooked up by our deluded mind. They may not be bad to begin with, and this is something that we fail to appreciate. If we only see badness in everyone and everything, the more miserable we become. Through learning this technique, we can use that in our waking hours so the next time we feel miserable, we can learn how to be happy with a more life-affirming attitude rather than being given to hopelessness, helplessness, depression, self loathing, and loathing of other people. That is the reason dream transformation is emphasized.

3. The third point mentioned is the notion of self-liberation where if we experience something terrifying, this time, we do not try to transform. We have learned to recognize, then we have learned to transform. Now, as the teachings describe it, even if we experience extremely bad scenarios where we think we are being murdered, kidnapped, or thrown into a dungeon, we

accept that. We say, "This is just a dream. It's a dream and I recognize it to be a dream," and we just accept what is happening. So you stay in the dungeon. If you are being carried along by a strong current, you do not freak out. You say, "This is a dream. It's happening and I accept that. It's just a dream." By taking this attitude and approach, the experience can become liberated.

These three points of dream yoga sum up the main aspects of the practice: recognition, transformation, and liberation. If we practice in this way, we can go deeper into ourselves. Then there is real integration taking place between our subtle body and our subtle states of mind. We can have experiences of clear light mind or the Buddha mind, as it is described. Before we attain total enlightenment, if we have had some taste of this experience, according to Buddhism, we will start having different kinds of dreams, those that are not karmic.

There are Tibetan lamas who have written whole texts based on their dreams. For example, the guru may appear and begin teaching. Because the practitioner has been doing dream yoga practice and has been able to maintain mindfulness and awareness while sleeping, upon awakening, the practitioner has good recollection of what was said. They recollect the teachings, record them, and may use them when teaching. According to Buddhism, even in dreams, we can have both "pure visions" and "impure visions." Most of the dream experiences consist of "impure visions" produced by karmic imprints but as we advance with the dream yoga practice, our dreams may become "pure visions." Then, what we experience in dreams becomes meaningful and tending toward aspects of awakening instead of ignorance.

Due to ignorance, confusion, and delusions, we have many yet to be discovered capacities and abilities. Through pure vision, many untapped abilities and capacities can be unleashed and manifest in the individual. There are many stories of Tibetan lamas having dreams and becoming transformed through them. When they awaken, they are a different person from who they were when they went to sleep. They have grown, developed, and matured so much in a short period of time. When they wake up, they have become a far more advanced human being than when they went to sleep. This is taken very seriously in Tibetan Buddhism. These kinds of realizations or attainments come directly from dream yoga practice. The practices we do while sleeping can be equally beneficial to those done or conducted in our waking hours.

Sometimes it is said that via sleeping and dreaming yoga compared to conventional meditation practices, we develop on the path in a different manner. When we go to sleep, just like when we die, the mind is supposed to slow down. As discussed earlier, the mind is more like a society of mind with many different states and levels of consciousness. There are both good and bad departments, some of which are hidden, others very easily accessed, some very active, others dormant. The mind is very complex. When we go to sleep, all these activities of the mind slow down. Because the mind is calmer when asleep, we have greater access to our natural state of being than while we are awake, when the mind is occupied with many different things. This provides us with a great opportunity. We may not be able to maintain such awareness every night during sleep but with some effort, we may gain more insight into how our mind works and what is really going on.

Trying to interpret dreams is not the most important thing. Of course, it is still important, but "interpret" means that we are moving from what is there, trying to understand what is there. In Buddhism, *what is there* is much more important than trying to interpret or *understand what is there* in our mind when we are dreaming. When we try to understand what is going on, we are working from a particular point of view using a conceptual framework. So the interpretation arises from a particular view, frame of reference, or perspective.

Often, even in our waking hours, we learn by simply watching and observing people or objects. Instead of always trying to make sense of what is going on, thinking, "I have to understand what's going on. I have to make sense of this," getting worked up and confused, if we are a little more relaxed and pay attention and are more observant, we end up learning so much more than always trying to conceptualize and put things into neat pigeonholes. In other words, we are continuously trying to fit things into our familiar conceptual categories but according to the Buddhist view, our familiar conceptual categories are a product of ignorance. The Buddhist view is quite radical in that sense, saying that we cannot trust these things as much as we do.

Chapter Eighteen

Supplemental Practices of Dream Yoga

Dream yoga is one of the main practices of Tantrism, along with illusory body yoga and mystic heat yoga. To support one's efforts, dream yoga is not something that we normally practice separately from the other yogas in Tantrism. If one does dream yoga practice with the help of mystic heat yoga, illusory body yoga, yoga of transference of consciousness, and yoga of the bardo, one would gain more benefit than if one were only doing dream yoga. This does not mean one should not perform dream yoga on its own. Of course, one can do that, but there is a meaningful and illuminating relationship between these different yogas.

In Buddhism, there is a need for varieties of techniques to deal with the complexity of our mind and our experiences. The practices deal with delusions and distortions that can arise when awake, while sleeping, during the death process, and they help with our many emotional states. All of these practices are extremely important, as our need to reduce suffering to enable us to lead a fulfilling life cannot be addressed easily or myopically. Instead of only meeting our intellectual or emotional needs for example, we need to have many needs satisfied in order to have a fulfilling and full life.

Body

Some physical needs in terms of doing yoga and pranayama and understanding the gross and subtle aspect of one's physicality are addressed within these practices. It is not about purely thinking in terms of our body shape or height. The physical considerations we often obsess about, such as our shape and physical health, do not necessarily go together. Thinness for example, does not necessarily mean someone is healthy. The practices are all about building body awareness.

In all of these yoga practices, Buddhism teaches about awareness, mindfulness, and coming into proper contact with oneself and one's mental and physical states. If we cannot do that within the practices, there is no doubt it will not work. It is as simple as that. Even if we get fixated, it still will not work. Therefore, body awareness is an important part of Buddhist practice. Even when we do shamatha practice, we emphasize the physical posture, the breathing aspect, how we breathe, the position of the head, and the alignment of the spine. Meditation is not simply about plopping oneself on a cushion and hoping for the best. With shamatha or tranquility meditation, there is a lot involved; understanding how to be in touch with one's body when one is in meditation, holding the posture properly, adjusting one's breath and focus, et cetera. When the mind is relaxed, it would fall more easily in sync with the physical posture and breathing pattern. If we are holding the posture with rigidity and tension, we will not breathe with ease. Breathing can be restricted when accompanied by a sense of anxiety or fear. These are important points to understand when we are practicing.

As part of dream yoga meditation therefore, we need to include other forms of Buddhist practice. We cannot simply do dream yoga practice, lie down and see if we can recognize, transform, or liberate our dreams. It is more about asking, "What other kinds of practices can I do to assist this process?" This is why practices like shamatha are so important because they are essential foundations to yogic exercises done in esoteric forms of Buddhism. The yogic exercises are based on that simple principle of shamatha. We do shamatha practice and yogic exercises not simply for the physical benefit, though there are many, but to avail us the opportunity for body mind integration, and generally be in a better frame of mind.

All forms of physical exercise and posture that we may adopt during meditation or yogic exercises are a means to an end. The end is to realize our true nature, which is called Buddha mind. This is the goal, but we do not have to ignore our physicality to realize that. As previously discussed, it is not the case that you go to sleep and only deal with the mind. You go to sleep and deal with mind and body using the visualization practices.

According to the tantric teachings, it is extremely difficult for us to truly integrate the body and mind without using visualization. I return to the point that our habitual way of thinking is conditioned by dualistic thought patterns. We need to keep returning to this notion. All the yogas emphasize that integration of body and mind is fundamental. Yoga in Buddhism is not simply about physical exercise. We bring mind into the practice through visualization and the use of deities and other images. Human beings are accustomed to using images in ordinary life and that is what grabs our attention. In a manner of speaking, it is where our thoughts and body meet.

According to Buddhism, our ability to imagine is based on the body and incidentally, the brain. The brain processes and chemicals in the body have an impact. This is addressed in terms of what Buddhists mean by "bindu" or "thigle," life essence. You could liken this to subtle physical or bodily chemistry. Due to dualistic way of thinking, we can forget about body awareness and real physical health. This is one point I wish to emphasize, using the body as an aid to one's spiritual development. If we want to do dream yoga practices, it is good to perform pranayama, yoga, tai chi, or other similar activities, and of course, sitting meditation.

We use our body to stabilize the mind. With shamatha practice, we might be thinking we want to stabilize our mind, but not equate that with our body—how we treat, view, and experience our body. We live in our bodies, after all. From an awareness perspective, we can become separated from our bodies with little sense of real embodiment. We have to remind ourselves that when we use the body, we are doing so in order to develop awareness and get in touch with ourselves and our sense of being.

Imagination

If we wish to do dream yoga, it is very important to appreciate the notion of using the imagination. Being able to imagine different images should not be dismissed as unimportant or optional. It is important to note that when we visualize, it includes the capacity to unlock the channels, the nadis, and so forth. Thinking about the practice and having strong feelings and emotions about the practice is not enough, but if we combine imagination with feelings and emotions, and the right thought processes and effort, then we can experience real transformation.

Otherwise, we might have strong feelings and emotions and without the other necessary elements, we may be transformed in the opposite direction. If we are not thinking in the right manner, we can become more and more confused and end up being stubborn and stagnant in how we view things.

In Buddhism, our patterns of thinking are described as being based on our view of the world. This idea comes up repeatedly in Buddhist teachings. For example, in early Buddhism, with the noble eightfold path, the first one is "right view." When we discuss Madhyamaka philosophy, it is the "middle view,"[55] the "five wrong views,"[56] and so forth. According to Tantrism, when we bring all these disparate elements of thinking, feeling, and emotions together, then we can imagine effectively. It is our imagination, being able to visualize. According to Buddhism, not many of us have a good imagination so we have to start with visualization. We have to visualize and then we can learn to imagine things properly. If we imagine in the right way, we will become transformed. That is how dream yoga and also deity yoga practice works.

Altruistic Mind

We need a good and caring mind to transform. If we do not have that and remain selfish and egocentric, one's intention for practice can be very misguided. One may think, "If only I could get that manual on how to do dream yoga, I could do it and really be advancing and show people how great I am." In the teachings, it discusses how a practitioner can get lost and become excessively self-absorbed. One can become absorbed in their own practice instead of thinking about the purpose of doing the practice. This happens often in life. For example, in the beginning, a successful businessperson may have set out to make a good living for the family, but after a while, making money becomes the number one concern and all other concerns fall by the wayside. That type of self-absorption can cause us to act purely out of the wish to be seen as an extremely successful person. Other ordinary and altruistic motives may fall by the wayside while business and money become the all-consuming goal.

When we do our practices, we should approach them with a sense of openness, compassion, and care. If we do that, we then feel connected to the rest of the world and other people. This does not mean that we have to feel connected to everybody. Just because one does not connect with one or two people does not mean it is a lost cause. According to Buddhism, feeling connected is more important than whether you believe you actually are connected with others. There is a distinction there. Throughout this section on dream yoga, I have been emphasizing different kinds of distinctions. Making these distinctions is important. Some distinctions are more important than others; "What is the most important thing in life and what is less important?" We have to learn to distinguish between the things that are truly important and those that are less so.

When we view it in this manner, we realize that being a nice person, more easy-going, and approachable is actually very important. According to Buddhist teachings, even in life on a mundane level, we will have better success with people because they will naturally be drawn to us rather than someone who is totally selfish. If somebody is rich and powerful, people may not be drawn to them because of who they are. In Buddhism, it does not say that a caring person has to be poor, but it does say that whether one is poor or rich, the importance of being a caring person remains very important.

To support our dream yoga practices, it is important and advisable to meditate and contemplate on the four immeasurables,[57] lojong or the seven points of mind training, and so on. It is important to feel that one is connected to others. If we feel that, when we do dream yoga, we are going to experience things in a different way. Fundamentally, we always adopt a viewpoint associated with a practice and look at things in a particular way. What we experience in life is dependent more on our viewpoint than what is actually going on. So if we are approaching everything with a better attitude and view of life, we are going to experience the benefits and rewards. But if we are approaching life and our practices with the wrong attitude and view, everything will fall short of what could be, might have been, or what is.

A caring attitude and a benevolent compassionate mind in Buddhism has a very wide connotation. It is not just about doing some good work for others, you have to take on board the whole idea of bodhicitta, the enlightened heart, as it is referred to in Buddhism, so that we learn to care in a much more fundamental way. It is not only about "doing," but it is also about being nice, friendly, and pleasant to others. This is even more important than *acting* friendly, compassionate, or benevolent, such as if you act compassionately, but do not feel. A genuinely caring attitude is not duty-bound. Learning to be a kinder is good thing. To be kinder or friendlier does not mean one has to become stupid and let others take advantage of you. Intelligent use of kindness is important and needs to be practiced.

Three Points to Gaining Knowledge and Wisdom

The first point, from the Buddhist point of view, is the importance of always continuing one's education. What we learn from Nagarjuna, for example, might help us in the long run, but what the latest celebrity says in a glossy magazine, on the other hand, may not. Reading books that are important is vital—not only Buddhist books, but books that are informative and have some substance. We should always seek to learn more, be it through ancient texts or books on contemporary issues. According to Buddhism, this is one aspect of the cultivation of wisdom. The wisdom that we gain from listening and reading is called *thos pa'i shes rab* in Tibetan.[58] Through reading and listening, we gain knowledge and wisdom.

The second point is knowledge gained from contemplation. In Buddhism, contemplation and meditation are different. When we contemplate, we think deeply and consider what we have read. We may often just read and intellectually understand something but not have digested it very much, similar to going to college or university and selecting a subject just to complete a course. The essays and other work may be done, but one has not considered or pondered over the new knowledge, and it can then be easily lost. If one truly takes what one has read seriously, it needs to be contemplated and thoroughly studied. For example, the philosopher Plato needs more than a quick read to develop a fuller understanding. It will help so much if we contemplate on what we have read.

In Buddhism, listening and reading is distinguished from contemplating and meditating. We may read but not retain much, but if we contemplate, much of it will stay in our mind. The next time we encounter a life experience and ask, "What should I do?" suddenly a voice pops up in our mind and says, "Plato has said one should do this in this circumstance." Then you think, "That's so true. That's absolutely right." That can be so helpful. With Buddhist texts, we should not rely solely on the commentaries, but also truly try to understand the author and the verses in the text. This would also serve us well.

The third point is meditation, which concerns meditating upon what we have read and contemplated. After contemplating and digesting Buddhist teachings and texts, we should meditate. According to Buddhism, we ordinarily think purely in conceptual terms. So if we do dream yoga and have some success recognizing the dreams while dreaming and transforming them, still, we are using the conceptual mind. Our innate wisdom is not yet fully engaged. For that to happen, we have to meditate. That is why in dream yoga, the notion of liberation is mentioned. With one of the practices, it is about letting the dream experiences arise and not being too worried about it and so one can experience or find the non-conceptual state.

Breaking through and into the transcendental state is extremely important in Buddhism because until we can do that, we are not really spiritual. We are still trapped in the empirical, almost secular, worldly state, but if we break through that, we are in the transcendental state. "Transcendental" in Buddhism is understood more in terms of one's own experience than reality itself. If we are talking about reality itself, we might say it is the experience of the transcendent. To put it simply, if we say "transcendental," in the Buddhist context, this means a state that is non-egoistic, non-self-centered. The experience of breaking through or transcending the

180 Vajrayana: An Essential Guide to Practice

confinement of our egoic perceptions comes from meditation.

Learning, contemplating, and meditating are activities we practice to accumulate wisdom. These are needed to be successful with dream yoga practice as well. There is no doubt that if we build awareness, have a more positive and friendly attitude, and develop a benevolent mind, with the three wisdom practices, mindfulness and awareness will arise. Mindfulness and awareness when studying the Dharma and other substantial topics will build depth and richness within our contemplations.

It is easy to misread or misinterpret what we read. We may be thinking, "That was so profound. It was so great." We may become quite proud and think, "I really understood that point so well." In discussing such matters with others or with further study, we may find our understanding was lacking and further investigation is needed. It is important to be open in that way and pursue thorough learning. If we have misunderstood or misinterpreted what was read and followed up with erroneous contemplations without mindfulness or awareness, it can lead to fixation and a reluctance to give up one's opinions, even when those opinions turn out to be groundless or weak. Our meditation will also be misdirected and misguided without proper understanding of the view associated with a particular practice. In Buddhism, we consider the relationship these activities have upon one another.

Buddhism says we should do certain practices, but there is the question, "Why should we do these practices?" I have attempted to explain why we should do them and why they are helpful, not only in terms of our spiritual practice, but also in terms of life generally. Doing these practices should make us better human beings. That is what we all want. We want to be better human beings but often, we do not know how to go about achieving that. It is important to build confidence in a whole body of tradition that provides the type of guidance that Buddhism is able to provide.

Such a comprehensive tradition I think can rightly command our respect. We may not have enough appreciation for the idea that when something has worked for a long time, it can still be relevant. For example, it seems to me that modern philosophers have not surpassed many of the points discussed by people such as Plato and Aristotle. We may want to be another Plato or Aristotle, but before we become another Plato or Aristotle, it is important to learn from past masters with a sense of deep appreciation and respect.

Up until now, all that the Buddha taught, all that the Buddha said, has withstood the test of time. Many followers have had genuine experiences as prescribed by the Buddha confirming his words through meditative experience. What can we have more than our own experiences to prove whether something is real or not? This is an important point. Of course, there has to be some kind of external criterion to judge whether an experience is genuine or not. Buddhism continues a tradition of thorough scrutiny through scholarship and debate. Buddhist ethics are also powerful and profound. Of course, there are Buddhists who follow Buddhism well and there are Buddhists who do not. By and large, Buddhists try to follow what the Buddha taught. They have not lost sight of the practice of temperance, moderation, the use of intellect, being kind to others, embracing change, learning to accept impermanence rather than fighting against it, and moving with the times. All of these are a part of Buddhist history.

There is such variety in Buddhism, more that we may find in some other traditions. If you go to a Theravada temple, it is very different from a Tibetan temple. There are also differences in language and cultural mores. That should be seen as a strength in Buddhism. Buddhism promotes certain values that allow for tremendous diversity.

If you have been Buddhist for many years, you must have a little faith. When we do not have faith and instead doubt everything excessively, we experience more problems and difficulties in life. How many years do we have to test the Dharma to prove that it does work? We will get a lot more out of the Dharma if we have faith in it. We may think dualistically, in black and white terms and say, "If I really believed in the Dharma, I would become a Buddhist fundamentalist!" Believing in somebody or something does not make us a fundamentalist. It means we have conviction, commitment, and a strong direction in our lives. What makes a fundamentalist? An inability to accept diversity can make us a fundamentalist. Believing that what somebody else believes in is evil can make us a fundamentalist.

As human beings, we need to believe in things. Not believing in anything can make our life directionless, less meaningful, and poorer. Even with material prosperity, our life can still feel hopeless. When we demonize others, this is when we become a fundamentalist. But there is nothing bad about believing in yourself, what you do, and what you cherish and value to be good. Why then take the next step and say that other people who do not share your views are terrible? Believing in what one is doing is good. Thinking that what is good is something we should cultivate or believe in is a positive way to live. In that way, choosing to be more compassionate and doing Buddhist practices will be worthwhile and meaningful.

Notes

SECTION ONE
OVERVIEW OF BUDDHIST TANTRA
Chapter One
Sutra and Tantra: differences between
Exoteric and Esoteric Buddhism

1. Conflicting emotions (Skt. *klesha*). The five main conflicting emotions are excessive anger, desire, jealousy, pride, and ignorance. Alternate terms for the conflicting emotions include; defiled emotions, afflictive emotions, and disturbing emotions.

2. Here, the terms "gods" and "goddesses" do not refer to external divine beings such as to be found in monotheistic religions. Rather, they reflect aspects of our true or enlightened nature. There are a variety of different gods and goddesses in Tibetan Buddhism, such as for example, the "dakinis" which are the female representation of enlightened energy and "dakas," the male equivalents.

3. "Divine" in this context can be defined as an experiential visualization of perfect quality or qualities represented within a deity or collection of deities, and other symbolic entities, individually and collectively demonstrating and disseminating such perfections as universal compassion, love, protection, clarity of mind, and so on.

4. A monad is a philosophical term adopted by the philosopher Gottfried Wilhelm Leibniz, who referenced the monad as an elementary particle. In brief according to Leibniz, monads are unitary, true, self-existing, and self-sufficient substances or mental states and thus exist without reference to any "other."

The Oxford Dictionary of Philosophy, Simon Blackburn, Oxford University press, NY, 1996.

Chapter Two
The Sutric Heritage in Tantra and the Clear Light Mind of Bliss

5. In brief, the Mahayana path has a spiritual perspective that seeks to gain enlightenment for the benefit of others, seen as a different perspective to seeking enlightenment for one's self and is known as the "path of purification," the "Bodhisattvayana," or the "Bodhisattva path." The development of both wisdom, through meditation, and compassion, through action and engagement in the world, are described as the two wings of a bird. The Mahayana tradition has two aspects, the sutric and tantric traditions of Mahayana. *Integral Buddhism: Developing all Aspect's One's Personhood*, Traleg Kyabgon, Shogam Publications, Australia, 2018.

6. Nagarjuna (150—250 CE) is commonly considered to be one of the most significant philosophers of Buddhism. He is seen as a founder of the Madhyamaka school of Mahayana Buddhism. *Mahayana Budhhism: the Doctrinal Foundations*, Paul Williams, Routledge, USA, 1999.

7. Buddhaghosa (fourth-fifth century) was an Indian Theravadin Buddhist philosopher and translator. He lived during the fifth century. *Dictionary of Religion in India*, Roshen Dalal, Penguin Books, India, 2006.

8. Dogen Zenji (1200—1253 CE) was a Japanese philosopher, Buddhist priest, and founder of the Soto school of Zen. *Zen Buddhism: the Origin of Wisdom*, O.B. Duane, Brookhampton Press, UK, 1988.

9. Padmasambhava was an Indian tantric Buddhist master who

is said to have contributed to the spread of Buddhism in Tibet and surrounding regions during the eighth century. He is also known as Guru Rinpoche. *The Adornment of the Middle Way*, Padmakara Translation Group, Shambhala, USA, 2010.

10. In philosophy, ontology is the study of being or what exists. *The Oxford Dictionary of Philosophy*, Simon Blackburn, Oxford University press, NY, 1996.

11. Asanga, (fourth century), seen as a significant spiritual teacher of Mahayana Buddhism and a founder of the Yogacara, Vijnanavada, or "mind only" school. *The Adornment of the Middle Way*, Padmakara Translation Group, Shambhala Publications, USA, 2010.

12. The six paramitas are generosity, patience, vigor, moral precepts, meditative concentration, and wisdom. *The Essence of Buddhism: an Introduction to its Philosophy and Practice*, Traleg Kyabgon, Shambhala Publications, USA, 2014.

13. The author commented that it is also not like the Christian notion that Jesus dwells within us.

Chapter Three
The Practice of Deity Yoga

14. Buddhism did not have a monopoly over Tantra on the Indian subcontinent. There are other forms of Tantra in India. Both Hindu and non-Hindu Tantra exist, and have existed, independently of the Buddhist tradition. Non-Hindu Tantra refers to Indian traditions that were neither Hindu nor Buddhist in origin. The author stated "I do not want to go into the historical origins of the tantric teachings, but many scholars have speculated that both Buddhist and Hindu Tantra have a common origin that was native to the Indian subcontinent." This existed prior to the Aryan invaders and therefore

constituted a native Indian religion that predates its recorded history.

15. Bodhicitta can be translated as enlightened heart. It has two aspects: relative bodhicitta and ultimate bodhicitta. Relative bodhicitta is compassion, and ultimate bodhicitta refers to the nature of the mind. *The Essence of Buddhism: an Introduction to its Philosophy and Practice*, Traleg Kyabgon, Shambhala Publications, USA, 2014.

16. The Gelug tradition is one of the four main schools of Tibetan Buddhism.

17. A heuristic approach is one that employs a useful method in order to reach a specific goal. *The Oxford Dictionary of Philosophy*, Simon Blackburn, Oxford University press, NY, 1996.

18. Chenrezig (Skt. *Avalokiteshvara*) represents the embodiment of love and compassion.

19. Manjushri represents transcendental wisdom and is associated with learning and music. *Meeting the Buddhas: a Guide to Buddhas, Bodhisattvas, and Tantric Deities*, Windhorse Publications, UK, 1993.

20. Tara is a significant female wisdom deity who has many forms. Her qualities include building a bridge of insight from samsara to nirvana. *Meeting the Buddhas: a Guide to Buddhas, Bodhisattvas, and Tantric Deities*, Windhorse Publications, UK, 1993.

21. The Buddhist approach to the human mind is what is called "non-essentialist" or "non-substantialist," (Skt. *anatman*). At the time the Buddha taught, Hindu philosophers and spiritual masters spoke about substances. They taught that the world is unreal but that Brahma has substance and inherently exists so

is therefore substantial, and that through contemplation, mental processes are revealed as temporary, but that there is something that is stable, permanent, eternal. They called it "atma" or soul.

Chapter Four
Empowerment and the Vajra Master

22. Dakpo Tashi Namgyal (1513–1587 CE) was a celebrated Tibetan Buddhist yogi and scholar. For more information see, *Moonbeams of Mahamudra: the Classic Meditation Manual*, Dakpo Tashi Namgyal; Traleg Kyabgon (translator), Shogam Publications, 2015.

23. Jetsun Milarepa (1052—1155 CE) is one of the most well known yogis in Tibetan literature. Milarepa endured many trials under his teacher, Marpa Lotsawa. He spent many years in forest retreat and is famous for the poetry known as "100,000 songs of Milarepa." *Meeting the Buddhas: a Guide to Buddhas, Bodhisattvas, and Tantric Deities*, Windhorse Publications, UK, 1993.

24. "Roshi" is generally considered to be a term of high respect given to the spiritual head of a Zen Buddhist community. This definition may vary between different sects.

Chapter Five
The Preparatory Arrangements for the Empowerment

25. The five Buddha families are associated with a specific emotion and have both a confused and enlightened aspect. The five emotions are excessive desire, anger, jealousy, pride, and ignorance. Their corresponding wisdoms are the wisdom of discrimination, the wisdom of dharmadhatu or the authentic state, the wisdom of accomplishment, the wisdom of

equanimity, and mirror-like wisdom, respectively. *Moonbeams of Mahamudra: the Classic Meditation Manual*, Dakpo Tashi Namgyal; Traleg Kyabgon (translator), Shogam Publications, 2015.

26. Regarding evil influences, it is not a requirement that one believes in evil spirits, demons, or devils when practicing tantra. If someone does believe in such influences and feels they can sense a type of presence that may be harmful, in that kind of situation, tantric methods can be very helpful. After being initiated into the tantric world, we no longer think of demons, evil spirits, and so forth as external. It is seen as a product of dualistic thinking. We may still feel we are going to be harmed by evil spirits. If we realize our own natural clear light of bliss, from the tantric point of view, all of these perceptions of evil will vanish. Normally, we perceive them from the samsaric point of view but, from a non-samsaric point of view, we can see demeaning influences such as these as self created. From a higher perspective, we do not experience these things so we do not need to take any measures to deal with them. However, when we do experience such things, Tantrism has many methods for helping overcome such fears and to engender a greater feeling of confidence.

Chapter Six
The Four Empowerments

27. "The five poisons" can also be referred to as the five emotions or the five conflicting emotions as discussed in note 25.

28. Further reading regarding "mind as such" or "reality as such," *The Influence of Yogacara on Mahmudra*, Traleg Kyabgon, KTD Publications, USA, 2010.

29. Vajrasattva is a deity associated with purification practices and

is one of the ngondro or preliminary practices in the Kagyu tradition and practiced in the other traditions.

30. Dependent arising (Skt. *pratityasamutpada*) is a philosophical term that purports the lack of inherent existence. It is also referred to as interdependent arising.

31. To practice union with a consort is called *karmamudra* and to use deity yoga as a way to experience the same thing is called *jnanamudra*. In this way, one is initiated into the practice of "union." This is what the third empowerment entails.

32. The Hevajra tantra emphasizes the completion stage and is considered to be a mother tantra and non-dual tantra. That is, the non-dual tantra balances both method and wisdom. *Meeting the Buddhas: a Guide to Buddhas, Bodhisattvas, and Tantric Deities*, Windhorse Publications, UK, 1993.

33. The Guhyasamaja tantra is described as being in the desire class of the father tantras. *Meeting the Buddhas: a Guide to Buddhas, Bodhisattvas, and Tantric Deities*, Windhorse Publications, UK, 1993.

34. Yamantaka is the wrathful form of the peaceful bodhisattva of wisdom, Manjushri. Yamantaka is known as the "destroyer of death."

Chapter Seven
The Creative-Imagination Stage

35. Refer to note 25.

36. The bardo is often referred to as the intermediate state within which there are many levels of consciousness. The Tibetan book of the dead describes how after physical death, consciousness goes through various stages of disassociation from the physical body. Once this process is complete, one

encounters the "clear light of bliss"—the dazzling radiance of ultimate reality. However, this experience can be too much for us so we turn away. From a taste of non-duality, we retreat into dualistic experience. Our consciousness reverts to its habitual interpretation of experience in terms of a subject confronted by external objects. If we recognize appearances for what they are, when in the bardo, we can begin to free ourselves from cyclic existence. *Meeting the Buddhas: a Guide to Buddhas, Bodhisattvas, and Tantric Deities*, Windhorse Publications, UK, 1993. *The Tibetan Book of the Dead: the Great Liberation Through Hearing in the Bardo*, Francesca Fremantle & Chögyam Trungpa, Shambhala Publications, USA, 1987.

Chapter Eight
Mystic Heat Yoga and the Completion Stage

37. Naropa (956—1040 CE) was a professor at Nalanda University in India and one of the masters of the Kagyu lineage. *The Essence of Buddhism: an Introduction to its Philosophy and Practice*, Traleg Kyabgon, Shambhala Publications, USA, 2014.

38. Emptiness (Skt. *shunyata*) means lack of inherent existence, or being empty of essence or substance. It refers to the lack of inherent existence in phenomena. The author in his book Essence of Buddhism, explains emptiness: "Understanding emptiness allows us to see the world as it is and not believe the world as it appears to our deluded mind. It does not mean that things do not exist. Just because things lack inherent existence or a permanent enduring essence does not mean they don't exist. The error is not in thinking that things exist but in thinking that things have some kind of substance that endures." Believing in enduring essence causes us to cling and grasp instead of retaining the necessary flexibility to accommodate

change. *The Essence of Buddhism: an Introduction to its Philosophy and Practice*, Traleg Kyabgon, Shambhala Publications, USA, 2014.

39. When giving a talk, the author referred to movement of psychophysical energy thus: "The consciousness attaches itself to the psychophysical energy or prana and to the life essence or bindu. According to Tantrism, thoughts have movement. We have our mood swings, which rise and fall and feelings that are also intense or dull, and this is related to the movement of the prana. If there is no movement in the psychophysical energy, then there is no movement in the mind; there will be no mental function. This is a view specific to Tantra, which says that even our sensory perceptions are determined by psychophysical energy. The idea is that, instead of trying to control our mind, if we learn how to work with our subtle body, then our mind will calm down automatically. Instead of trying to tackle the thoughts and emotions that we experience directly, if we work with our subtle energies, our thoughts and emotions will subside and our level of agitation will diminish."

Chapter Nine
The Completion Stage Practices

40. Mahasiddha Tilopa (998—1069 CE) lived in India. His main disciple was Naropa. Tilopa is one of masters of the Kagyu lineage, revered by all the main schools of Tibetan Buddhism. *Tilopa's Wisdom: His Life and Teachings on the Ganges Mahamudra*, Khenchen Thrangu, Snow Lion, USA, 2019.

SECTION TWO
THE SIX YOGAS OF NAROPA
Chapter Ten
Overview of the Six Yogas of Naropa

41. Marpa Lotsawa, Jetsun Milarepa, and Gampopa are considered part of the lineage of the Kagyu School of Tibetan Buddhism. Phagmo Drupa was a disciple of Gampopa.

42. The author mentioned how the practices of dream yoga and illusory body yoga were originally one practice and became separated, and also that another yoga, "projected consciousness yoga" has been lost: "I should mention here that during an earlier period, the Six Yogas consisted of mystic heat yoga, yoga of clear light, illusory body yoga, the yoga of transference of consciousness, the yoga of bardo, and what is called "projected consciousness yoga."

Chapter Eleven
Mystic Heat Yoga (Tummo)

43. Vajrayogini is a female diety depicted in semi-wrathful and wrathful forms, or in union with Chakrasamvara, et cetera. Vajrayogini practices predominate in the Kagyu tradition, but are also practiced in all the major schools. *Vajrayogini: Her Visualizations, Rituals, and Forms*, Elizabeth English, Wisdom Publications, USA, 2002.

44. Chakrasamvara is an important yidam in the Kagyu school, but also in all the major schools. The Chakrasamvara practice in general, is considered to have begun through the Indian siddha Saraha. Chakrasamvara is a central deity in the Mother tantra class and he appears in a number of different forms. *Meeting the Buddhas: a Guide to Buddhas, Bodhisattvas, and Tantric Deities*, Windhorse Publications, UK, 1993. *The*

Tibetan Book of the Dead: the Great Liberation Through Hearing in the Bardo, Francesca Fremantle & Chögyam Trungpa, Shambhala Publications, USA, 1987.

Chapter Thirteen
Dream Yoga

45. The alayavijnana or storehouse consciousness is a subtle level of consciousness where karmic imprints are stored as seeds and then mature into experience. It is similar to the western psychological notion of the unconscious. The alayavijnana concept is an important philosophical aspect of the Yogacara school. *The Influence of Yogacara on Mahmudra*, Traleg Kyabgon, KTD Publications, USA, 2010.

46. "Dream-like" (Tib. *milam tabu*; Wyl. *rmi lam lta bu*).

Chapter Fourteen
Clear Light Yoga, Yoga of Bardo, and Transference of Consciousness

47. Emptiness & empty (Tib. & Wyl. *stongs pa*).

SECTION THREE
DREAM YOGA
Chapter Fifteen
Illusion and Reality

48. Marpa (eleventh century) was known as Marpa the translator. Through his efforts, he managed to preserve the authenticity of the Buddhist teachings given to him by Naropa of India. Marpa brought back these teachings from India to Tibet and was credited with reigniting Buddhism that had waned at that time in Tibet. Marpa's main disciple was Milarepa. *The Life of Marpa the Translator*, Nalanda Translation Committee, Shambhala Publications, USA, 1995.

49. Mind training or *lojong* can be translated as cultivating compassion through training the mind. The collection of penetrating Dharma slogans is central to the study and contemplation of these teachings designed to develop compassion, equanimity, loving-kindness, and joy for others. These sets of teachings highlight the practice of bodhichitta, or enlightened heart, and were introduced to Tibet in the eleventh century. *The Practice of Lojong: Cultivating Compassion Through Training the Mind*, Traleg Kyabgon, Shambhala Publications, USA, 2007.

Chapter Sixteen
Philosophy of Dream Yoga

50. Storehouse consciousness or fundamental consciousness (Skt. alayavijnana; Tib. & Wyl. *kun gzhi rnam shes*).

51. Functionalism in western philosophy states that what makes something a mental state depends solely on its function or role. It is seen as the modern successor to behaviorism developed by such researchers as Ivan Pavlov. *The Oxford Dictionary of Philosophy*, Simon Blackburn, Oxford University press, NY, 1996.

Chapter Seventeen
The Practices of Dream Yoga

52. In the author's book *The Essence of Buddhism*, tranquility or shamatha meditation is described thus: It teaches us how to become settled and calm and to concentrate so that our minds are not always reaching out, grabbing onto this and that, and becoming scattered. We learn how to focus our mind, to become centered. We also learn how to be present and not to dwell on our past achievements, failures, regrets, or guilt associated with all kinds of things we may have done or failed

to do. Indulging in these many mental activities without focus one can lose perspective and react to things more and more from a habitual responsiveness rather than from clear understanding. In this way we can learn to be attentive and more present. In meditation when thoughts or emotions arise we try to let them go and not dwell on them. We usually use the breath as our point of concentration to return to if the mind wanders. Shamatha is in part the art of resting without judgment. As the many activities subside and the mind remains less disturbed and distracted, it provides the opportunity for wisdom to arise. *The Essence of Buddhism: an Introduction to its Philosophy and Practice*, Traleg Kyabgon, Shambhala Publications, USA, 2014.

53. The letter "AH" in the Tibetan alphabet is: ཨ

54. The unity of appearance and reality (Tib. & Wyl. *snang stong zung 'jug*).

Chapter Eighteen
Supplemental Practices of Dream Yoga

55. Madhyamaka literally means "the middle way." It is a school of Mahayana Buddhism founded by Nagarjuna and Aryadeva and emphasizes the doctrine of emptiness. The middle way describes the position taken by its adherents in relation the existence or non-existence of things. Madhyamaka uses elaborate reasoning to show that things do not have any enduring essence. *The Adornment of the Middle Way: Shantarakshita's Madhyamakalankara*, Padmakara Translation Group, Shambhala Publications, USA, 2005.

56. There are five "wrong views" in Abhidharma literature that belong to the subgroup of the six root destructive emotions. The five wrong views are: the view that the self (or sense of "I"

or "me") is both permanent and separate to our memories, emotions, thoughts, and attitudes, et cetera; extremist views of eternalism and nihilism; views that cut to the roots or obstruct virtuous thought and activity; belief in ideological supremacy, and finally, belief in ethical and ritual supremacy. *The Essence of Buddhism: an Introduction to its Philosophy and Practice*, Traleg Kyabgon, Shambhala Publications, USA, 2014. https://www.rigpawiki.org/index.php?title=Wrong_view

57. The author in his book, Mind at Ease (Luminous Bliss), describes the four immeasurables or Brahmaviharas. They are practices specifically designed to bring about the type of feelings, emotions, and thoughts that will have a positive effect on our character. Meditating on the four immeasurables, that of love, compassion, joy, and equanimity, provides the opportunity to re-orientate ourselves and transcend our limited egocentric self-absorbed state of being. *Luminous Bliss: Self-realisation Through Meditation*, Traleg Kyabgon, Shogam Publications, Australia, 2019. *Mind at Ease: Self-liberation Through Mahamudra Meditation*, Shambhala Publications, USA, 2004.

58. Wisdom that we gain from listening and reading (Tib. & Wyl. *thos pa'i shes rab*).

Index